lonely planet

Fast Talk

Thai

Guaranteed to get you talking

T0103434

Contents

⇒ Special Features

Before You Go

Cradled between Cambodia, Laos, Malaysia, and Myanmar, the Kingdom of Thailand is something of a Tower of Babel, with numerous dialects spoken. What's known as Standard Thai is actually a dialect spoken in Bangkok and the surrounding provinces. It's the official language of administration, education and the media, and most Thais understand it even if they speak another dialect. All the words and phrases in this book are translated into Standard Thai.

PRONUNCIATION TIPS

Just about all of the sounds in Thai exist in English. While some people may find it difficult to pronounce Thai words, persistence is the key. Locals will appreciate your efforts and often help you along.

★ Most consonants in our phonetic system are pronounced the same as in English but Thai does has a few tricky consonants. Watch out for the Þ sound which is halfway between a 'b' and a 'p', and the đ sound which is halfway between a 'd' and a 't'.

★ In this book we have used hyphens to separate syllables from each another. So the word ang-grìt (English) is made up of two distinct syllables ang and grìt. In some words we have divided the syllables further with a dot · in order to help you separate vowel sounds and avoid mispronunciation. So the word kĕe·an is actually pronounced as one syllable with two separate vowel sounds.

MUST-KNOW GRAMMAR

★ The pronoun 'I' will change depending on the gender of the speaker – so a man will refer to himself as pŏm ผม (I, me) while a

4

woman will refer to herself as dì-chăn ดิฉัน (I, me). When being polite to others, it's customary to add the word kráp ครับ (if you're a man) or kâ ค่ะ (if you're a woman) as a kind of a 'softener' to the end of questions and statements.

★ Often you'll see the symbol m/f in this book which stands for male/female. Whenever a sentence is marked with m/f you have to make a choice between pŏm or dì-chăn or kráp and kâ depending on your gender.

PLUNGE IN!

Don't be discouraged if Thai seems difficult at first – this is only because we aren't used to pronouncing certain Thai sounds the way we do in English. Speak slowly and follow the coloured phonetic guides next to each phrase. If you absolutely can't make yourself understood, simply point to the Thai phrase and show it to the person you're speaking to. The most important thing is to laugh at your mistakes and keep trying.

Fast Talk Thai

Don't worry if you've never learnt Thai (ภาษาไทย pah-săh tai) before – it's all about confidence. You don't need to memorise endless grammatical details or long lists of vocabulary – you just need to start speaking. You have nothing to lose and everything to gain when the locals hear you making an effort. And remember that body language and a sense of humour have a role to play in every culture.

"you just need to start speaking"

Even if you use the very basics, such as greetings and civilities, your travel experience will be the better for it. Once you start, you'll be amazed how many prompts you'll get to help you build on those first words. You'll hear people speaking, pick up sounds and expressions from the locals, catch a word or two that you know from TV already, see something on a billboard – all these things help to build your understanding.

5. Phrases to Learn Before You Go

1. Have you eaten?
กินข้าวหรือยัง

gin kôw rĕu yang

In Thailand instead of asking 'What are you up to?', it's customary to ask 'Have you eaten?'.

2. Please take off your shoes.
กรุณาถอดรองเท้า

gà-rú-nah tòrt rorng tów

Shoes are always removed when entering a house and this also applies to religious buildings.

3. Can you recommend a local speciality?
แนะนำอาหารรสเด็ดๆของแถวนี้ได้ไหม

náa-nam ah-hăhn rót dèt dèt kŏrng tăa·ou née dâi măi

Thailand's seemingly endless variety of local dishes is a major draw for visitors

4. Can you lower the price?
ลดราคาได้ไหม

lót rah-kah dâi măi

Bargaining is common in street markets and some small shops.

5. How do you say ...?
... ว่าอย่างไร

... wâh yàhng rai

If in doubt about a word or phrase, just ask.

10. Phrases to Sound Like a Local

Hey!	เฮ้ย	hêr·i
Great!	ยอด	yôrt
Sure.	แน่นอน	nâa norn
Maybe.	บางที	bahng tee
No way!	ไม่มีทาง	mâi mee tahng
Just a minute.	เดี๋ยวก่อน	dĕe·o gòrn
It's OK.	ไม่เป็นไร	mâi ben rai
No problem.	ไม่มีปัญหา	mâi mee ban-hăh
Oh, no!	ตายแล้ว	đai láa·ou
Oh my god!	คุณพระช่วย	kun prá chôo·ay

10. Phrases to Start a Sentence

When's (the next bus)?	(รถเมล์คันต่อไป) มาเมื่อไร (rót mair kan dòr ɓai) mah mêu·a rai
Where's (the market)?	(ตลาด) อยู่ที่ไหน (dà-làht) yòo têe nǎi
How much is it (per night)?	(คืนละ) เท่าไร (keun lá) tôw-rai
Could I have (the key), please?	ขอ (กุญแจห้อง) หน่อย kǒr (gun-jaa hôrng) nòy
I'd like to buy (an adaptor plug).	อยากจะซื้อ (ปลั๊กต่อ) yàhk jà séu (ɓlák dòr)
I'd like (the menu), please.	ขอ (รายการอาหาร) หน่อย kǒr (rai gahn ah-hǎhn) nòy
Can I take a photo (of you)?	ถ่ายรูป (คุณ) ได้ไหม tài rôop (kun) dâi mǎi
I need a (bottle opener).	ต้องการ (เครื่องเปิดขวด) dôrng gahn (krêu·ang ɓèut kòo·at)
I'm going to (Ayuthaya).	ผม/ดิฉันกำลังไป (อยุธยา) pǒm/dì-chǎn gam-lang ɓai (à-yút-tá-yal
I like dancing.	ผม/ดิฉันชอบ (เต้นรำ) pǒm/dì-chǎn chôrp (dên ram) m/f

8

Chatting & Basics

⟩ Fast Phrases

Hello.	สวัสดี sà-wàt-dee
Goodbye.	ลาก่อน lah gòrn
Do you speak English?	คุณพูดภาษาอังกฤษได้ไหม kun pôot pah-săh ang-grìt dâi măi

Essentials

Yes.	ใช่ châi
No.	ไม่ mâi
Please.	ขอ kŏr
Thank you (very much).	ขอบคุณ(มาก ๆ) kòrp kun (mâhk mâhk)
You're welcome.	ยินดี yin dee
Excuse me. (to get attention)	ขอโทษ kŏr tôht

Fast Talk

Pronunciation

Just about all of the sounds in Thai exist in English. While some people may find it difficult to pronounce Thai words, persistence is the key. Locals will appreciate your efforts and often help you along. Smile, point and try again. You'll be surprised how much sense you can convey with just a few useful words

Vowel sounds

Symbol	English equivalent	Example
a	run	bàt
aa	bad	gàa
ah	father	gah
ai	aisle	jài
air	flair	wair-lah
e	bed	ɓen
i	bit	ɓìt
ee	see	ɓee
eu	her or french bleu	beu
ew	new with rounded lips	néw
o	hot	bòt
oh	note	đoh
or	for	pôr
u	put	sùk
oo	moon	kôo
ou	o plus u, similar to the the o in old	láa·ou
ow	cow	bow
oy	boy	soy

Tones

If you listen to someone speaking Thai you'll notice that some vowels are pronounced at a high or low pitch while others swoop or glide in a sing-song manner. This is because Thai uses a system of carefully pitched tones to make distinctions between words. There are five distinct tones in Thai: mid, low, falling, high and rising. The accent marks above the vowel remind you which to use. The mid tone has no accent.

Consonant Sounds

Symbol	English equivalant	Example
b	**b**ig	bòr
ɓ	ri**b-p**unch	ɓlah
ch	**ch**art	chìng
d	**d**og	dèk
đ	har**d-t**imes	đòw
f	**f**ull	făh
g	**g**et	gài
h	**h**at	hèep
j	**j**unk	jahn
k	**k**ite	kài
l	**l**ike	ling
m	**m**at	máh
n	**n**ut	nŏo
ng	si**ng**	ngoo
p	**p**ush	pahn
r	**r**at	reu·a
s	**s**it	săh-lah
t	**t**ap	tów
w	**w**atch	wat
y	**y**es	yàhk

Excuse me. (to get past)	ขออภัย kŏr à-pai
Sorry.	ขอโทษ kŏr tôht

Language Difficulties

Do you speak English?	คุณพูดภาษาอังกฤษได้ไหม kun pôot pah-săh ang-grìt dâi măi
Does anyone speak English?	มีใครพูดภาษาอังกฤษได้บ้างไหม mee krai pôot pah-săh ang-grìt dâi bâhng măi
Do you understand?	คุณเข้าใจไหม kun kôw jai măi
Yes, I do.	ครับ/ค่ะเข้าใจ kráp/kâ, kôw jai m/f
No, I don't.	ไม่เข้าใจ mâi kôw jai
I speak a little.	พูดได้นิดหน่อย pôot dâi nít nòy

PHRASE BUILDER

Could you please ...?	... ได้ไหม	... dâi măi
repeat that	พูดอีกที	pôot èek tee
speak more slowly	พูดช้าๆ	pôot cháa cháa
write it down	เขียนลงให้	kĕe·an long hâi

PHRASE BUILDER

How do you ...?	...อย่างไร	... yàhng rai
pronounce this	ออกเสียง	òrk sĕe·ang
write 'Saraburi'	เขียนสระบุรี	kĕe·an sà·rà·bù·ree

Greetings

Hi.	หวัสดี	wàt·dee
Good day.	สวัสดี	sà·wàt·dee
Good night.	ราตรีสวัสดิ์	rah·đree sà·wàt
See you later.	เดี๋ยวพบกันใหม่	dĕe·o póp gan mài
Goodbye.	ลาก่อน	lah gòrn
How are you?	สบายดีไหม	sà·bai dee măi
Fine. And you?	สบายดี ครับ/ค่ะ แล้วคุณล่ะ	sà·bai dee kráp/kâ, láa·ou kun lâ m/f

Titles

Mr	นาย	nai
Ms/Mrs	น้า	nahng
Miss	น้าสาว	nahng sŏw

13

Fast Talk

Starting Off

When starting to speak another language, your biggest hurdle is saying aloud what may seem to be just a bunch of sounds. The best way to do this is to memorise a few key words, like 'hello', 'thank you' and 'how much?', plus at least one phrase that's not essential, eg 'how are you', 'see you later' or 'it's very cold/hot' (people love to talk about the weather!). This will enable you to make contact with the locals, and when you get a reply and a smile, it'll also boost your confidence.

Introductions

What's your name?	คุณชื่ออะไร
	kun chêu à-rai
My name is ...	ผม/ดิฉัน ชื่อ ...
	pŏm/dì-chăn chêu ... m/f

PHRASE BUILDER

This is my ...	นี่คือ ... ของ ผม/ดิฉัน	nêe keu ... kŏrng
		pŏm/dì-chăn m/f
child	ลูก	lôok
colleague	เพื่อนงาน	pêu·an ngahn
friend	เพื่อน	pêu·an
husband	ผัว	pŏo·a
partner (intimate)	แฟน	faan
wife	เมีย	mee·a

14

I'd like to introduce you to ...	นี่คือ ... nêe keu ...
I'm pleased to meet you.	ยินดีที่ได้รู้จัก yin-dee têe dâi róo jàk
Here's my ...	นี่คือ ... ของ ผม/ดิฉัน nêe keu ... kŏrng pŏm/ dì-chăn m/f

PHRASE BUILDER

What's your ...?	... ของคุณคืออะไร	... kŏrng kun keu à-rai
address	ที่อยู่	têe yòo
email address	ที่อยู่อีเมล	têe yòo ee-men
phone number	เบอร์โทรศัพท์	beu toh-rá-sàp

Personal Details

Where are you from?	คุณมาจากไหน kun mah jàhk năi

PHRASE BUILDER

I'm from ...	ผม/ดิฉัน มาจาก ประเทศ	pŏm/dì-chăn mah jàhk brà-têt ... m/f
Australia	ออสเตรเลีย	or-sà-drair-lee·a
Canada	แคนาดา	kaa-nah-dah
New Zealand	ประเทศนิวซีแลนด์	prà-têt new see- laan
the UK	อังกฤษ	ang-krìt
the USA	สหรัฐอเมริกา	sà-hà-rát à-mair- rí-gah

15

Local Knowledge

wâi me?

Although Western codes of behaviour are becoming more familiar in Thailand, the country still has its own proud traditions. One of these is the wâi ไหว้, the prayer-like gesture of hands held together in front of the chin, which is used in everyday interactions. The wâi is generally used in situations where Westerners would shake hands. Thus you would wâi when meeting a person for the first time, and also when meeting a person after an absence, or for the first time for that day. A wâi is always called for when meeting a person older than you or with a respected social position. Usually the younger person is expected to wâi first.

I'm married	ผม/ดิฉันแต่งงานแล้ว pŏm/dì-chăn đaang ngahn láa·ou
I'm not married	ผม/ดิฉันยังไม่แต่งงาน pŏm/dì-chăn yang mâi đaang ngahn
I'm separated	ผม/ดิฉันหย่ากันแล้ว pŏm/dì-chăn yàh gan láa·ou
I'm single	ผม/ดิฉันเป็นโสดอยู่ pŏm/dì-chăn ɓen sòht yòo

Age

How old are you?	คุณ อายุเท่าไร kun ah-yú tôw-rai
I'm ... years old.	ฉันอายุ ... ปี chăn ah-yú ... ɓee

How old is your daughter?	ลูกสาวของคุณอายุเท่าไร
	lôok sŏw kŏrng kun ah-yú tôw-rai
How old is your son?	ลูกชายของคุณอายุเท่าไร
	lôok chai kŏrng kun ah-yú tôw-rai
He/She is ... years old.	เขาอายุ ... ปี
	kŏw ah-yú ... bee

Occupations & Study

What's your occupation?	คุณมีอาชีพอะไร
	kun mee ah-chêep à-rai
I work in (administration)	ฉันทำงานทางด้าน(บริหาร)
	chăn tam ngahn tahng dâhn (bor-rí-hăhn)
I'm retired	ฉันปลดเกษียณแล้ว
	chăn blòt gà-sěe·an láa·ou
I'm unemployed	ฉันว่างงาน
	chăn wâhng ngahn

PHRASE BUILDER

I'm a ...	ฉันเป็น ...	chăn ben ...
civil servant	ข้าราชการ	kâh râht-chá-gahn
farmer	ชาวไร่	chow râi
journalist	นักข่าว	nák kòw
teacher	ครู	kroo

What are you studying? คุณกำลังเรียนอะไรอยู่
kun gam-lang ree·an à-rai
yòo

PHRASE BUILDER

I'm studying ...	ผม/ดิฉันกำลังเรียน ...	pŏm/dì-chăn gam-lang ree·an ... m/f
humanities	มนุษยศาสตร์	má-nút-sà-yá-sàht
science	วิทยาศาสตร์	wít-tá-yah-sàht
Thai	ภาษาไทย	pah-săh tai

Interests

What do you do in your spare time? คุณทำอะไรเวลาว่าง
kun tam à-rai wair-lah wâhng

Do you like ...? ชอบ ... ไหม
chôrp ... măi

PHRASE BUILDER

I (don't) like ...	ผม/ดิฉัน (ไม่) ชอบ ...	pŏm/dì-chăn (mâi) chôrp ... m/f
cooking	ทำอาหาร	tam ah-hăhn
dancing	เต้นรำ	đên ram
music	ดนตรี	don-đree
socialising	การสังคม	gahn săng-kom
travelling	การท่องเที่ยว	gahn tôrng têe·o
watching TV	ดูโทรทัศน์	doo toh-rá-tát

18

Feelings

Are you ...? คุณ ... ไหม
kun ... mǎi

PHRASE BUILDER

I'm (not) ...	ผม/ดิฉัน (ไม่) ...	pŏm/dì-chăn (mâi) ... m/f
cold	หนาว	nǒw
happy	ดีใจ	dee jai
hungry	หิว	hěw
in a hurry	รีบร้อน	rêep rórn
sad	เศร้า	sôw
thirsty	หิวน้ำ	hěw nám
tired	เหนื่อย	nèu·ay

Numbers

1	หนึ่ง	nèung
2	สอง	sǒrng
3	สาม	sǎhm
4	สี่	sèe
5	ห้า	hâh
6	หก	hòk
7	เจ็ด	jèt
8	แปด	bàat
9	เก้า	gôw
10	สิบ	sìp

11	สิบเอ็ด	sìp-èt
12	สิบสอง	sìp-sŏrng
13	สิบสาม	sìp-săhm
14	สิบสี่	sìp-sèe
15	สิบห้า	sìp-hâh
16	สิบหก	sìp-hòk
17	สิบเจ็ด	sìp-jèt
18	สิบแปด	sìp-bàat
19	สิบเก้า	sìp-gôw
20	ยี่สิบ	yêe-sìp
21	ยี่สิบเอ็ด	yêe-sìp-èt
30	สามสิบ	săhm-sìp
40	สี่สิบ	sèe-sìp
50	ห้าสิบ	hâh-sìp
100	หนึ่งร้อย	nèung róy
1,000	หนึ่งพัน	nèung pan
1,000,000	หนึ่งล้าน	nèung láhn

Time

What time is it?	กี่โมงแล้ว
	gèe mohng láa·ou
12 midnight	หกทุ่ม/เที่ยงคืน
	hòk tûm/têe·ang keun
12 noon	เที่ยง
	têe·ang

Fast Talk

Thai Time

In Thailand you may hear a person who arrives late for an appointment joke about being on 'Thai time' as punctuality is generally a more fluid concept than some Westerners are used to. But there is a specifically Thai way of telling the time which you'll need to learn if you want to avoid being late yourself.

The day is broken up into four periods. From midnight to six in the morning times begin with the word dèe ตี (strike), from six in the morning until midday they end with the word chów เช้า (morning), from midday to six in the evening they begin with the word bai บ่าย (afternoon) and from six in the evening until midnight they end with the word tûm ทุ่ม (thump).

Days

Monday	วันจันทร์ wan jan
Tuesday	วันอังคาร wan ang-kahn
Wednesday	วันพุธ wan pút
Thursday	วันพฤหัสบดี wan pá-réu-hàt
Friday	วันศุกร์ wan sùk
Saturday	วันเสาร์ wan sŏw
Sunday	วันอาทิตย์ wan ah-tít

21

Months

January	เดือนมกราคม	deu·an má-gà-rah-kom
February	เดือนกุมภาพันธ์	deu·an gum-pah-pan
March	เดือนมีนาคม	deu·an mee-nah-kom
April	เดือนเมษายน	deu·an mair-săh-yon
May	เดือนพฤษภาคม	deu·an préut-sà-pah-kom
June	เดือนมิถุนายน	deu·an mí-tù-nah-yon
July	เดือนกรกฎาคม	deu·an gà-rák-gà-dah-kom
August	เดือนสิงหาคม	deu·an sĭng-hăh-kom
September	เดือนกันยายน	deu·an gan-yah-yon
October	เดือนตุลาคม	deu·an đù-lah-kom
November	เดือนพฤศจิกายน	deu·an préut-sà-jì-gah-yon
December	เดือนธันวาคม	deu·an tan-wah-kom

Dates

What date is it today?	วันนี้วันที่เท่าไร	wan née wan têe tôw-rai

PHRASE BUILDER

last ...	...ที่แล้ว	... tee láa·ou
month	เดือน	deu·an
week	อาทิตย์	ah-tít
year	ปี	bee

It's (27 September).	วันที่(ยี่สิบเจ็ดเดือนกันยายน)	wan têe (yêe-sìp-jèt deu·an gan-yah-yon)
last night	เมื่อคืนนี้	mêu·a keun née
next ...	...หน้า	... nâh

PHRASE BUILDER

yesterday ...	...เมื่อวาน	... mêu·a wahn
afternoon	บ่าย	bài
evening	เย็น	yen
morning	เช้า	chów

Weather

What's the weather like?	อากาศเป็นอย่างไร ah-gàht ben yàhng rai?
What will the weather be like tomorrow?	พรุ่งนี้อากาศจะเป็นอย่างไร prûng-née ah-gàht jà ben yàhng rai?

23

PHRASE BUILDER

It's ...	มัน...	man ...
cold	หนาว	nŏw
flooding	กำลังน้ำท่วม	gam-lang nám tôo·am
hot	ร้อน	rórn
raining	มีฝน	mee fŏn
sunny	แดดจ้า	dàat jâh
warm	อุ่น	ùn
windy	มีลม	mee lom

Directions

Where's (the tourist office)?	(สำนักงานท่องเที่ยว) อยู่ที่ไหน (săm-nák ngahn tôrng têe·o) yòo têe năi
Which way is ...?	...อยู่ทางไหน ... yòo tahng năi

PHRASE BUILDER

It's ...	อยู่ ...	yòo ...
behind ...	ที่หลัง ...	têe lăng ...
in front of ...	ตรงหน้า ...	drong nâh ...
near ...	ใกล้ ๆ ...	glâi glâi ...
next to ...	ข้าง ๆ ...	kâhng kâhng ...
opposite	ตรงกันข้าม ...	drong gan kâhm ...
straight ahead	ตรงไป	drong bai

How far is it?	อยู่ไกลเท่าไร yòo glai tôw-rai?
Could you please write it down?	เขียนลงให้ได้ไหม kěe·an long hâi dâi măi?
Can you show me (on the map)?	ให้ดูในแผนที่ได้ไหม hâi doo (nai pǎn têe) dâi măi?
✂ **What's the address?**	ที่อยู่คืออะไร têe yòo keu à-rai?

PHRASE BUILDER

Turn ...	เลี้ยว...	lée·o ...
at the corner	ตรงหัวมุม	drong hŏo·a mum
left	ซ้าย	sái
right	ขวา	kwǎh

north	ทิศเหนือ tít něu·a
south	ทิศใต้ tít dâi
east	ทิศตะวันออก tít đà-wan òrk
west	ทิศตะวันตก tít đà-wan đòk

CHATTING & BASICS

25

Airports & Transport

≡ Fast Phrases

When's the next bus?	รถเมล์คันต่อไปมาเมื่อไร rót mair kan đòr bai mah mêu·a rai
Does this (train) stop at ...?	(รถไฟ) นี้จอดที่...ไหม (rót fai) née jòrt têe...măi
One ticket to ..., please.	ขอตั๋วไป...หนึ่งตั๋ว kor đoo·a bai...neung đoo·a

At the Airport

I'm on business.	ผม/ดิฉัน มาธุระ pŏm/dì-chăn mah tú-rá m/f
I'm on holiday.	ผม/ดิฉัน มาพักผ่อน pŏm/dì-chăn mah pák pòrn m/f

PHRASE BUILDER

I'm here for ...	ผม/ดิฉัน มาพักที่นี้ ...	pŏm/dì-chăn mah pák têe née ... m/f
(10) days	(สิบ) วัน	(sìp) wan
(two) months	(สอง) เดือน	(sŏrng) deu·an

ศุลกากร	sŭn-lá-gah-gorn	**Customs**
ปลอดภาษี	blòrt pah-sĕe	**Duty-Free**
กองตรวจคนเข้าเมือง	gorng đròo·at kon kôw meu·ang	**Immigration**
ด่านตรวจหนังสือเดินทาง	dàhn đròo·at năng- sĕu deun tahng	**Passport Control**

I have nothing to declare.	ไม่มีอะไรที่จะแจ้ง mâi mee à-rai têe jà jâang
I have something to declare.	มีอะไรที่จะต้องแจ้ง mee à-rai têe jà đôrng jâang
Do you have this form in (English)?	มีแบบฟอร์ม เป็นภาษาอังกฤษไหม mee bàap form ben pahsăh ang-grìt măi

Getting Around

What time does it leave?	ออกกี่โมง òrk gèe mohng

PHRASE BUILDER

When's the ... bus?	รถเมล์ คัน ...มาเมื่อไร	rót mair kan ... mah mêu·a rai
first	แรก	râak
last	สุดท้าย	sùt tái
next	ต่อไป	đòr bai

27

| How long does the trip take? | การเดินทางใช้เวลานานเท่าไร
gahn dern tahng chái
wair·lah nahn tôw rai |
| Is it a direct route? | เป็นทางตรงไหม
ƀen tahng đrong măi |

Buying Tickets

| Where do I buy a ticket? | ต้องซื้อตั๋วที่ไหน
đôrng séu đŏo·a têe năi |

PHRASE BUILDER

Can I have a ... ticket (to Chiang Mai)?	ขอตั๋ว ...ไป (เชียงใหม่)	kŏr đŏo·a ...ƀai (chee·ang mài)
1st-class	ชั้นหนึ่ง	chán nèung
2nd-class	ชั้นสอง	chán sŏrng
child's	สำหรับเด็ก	săm-ràp dèk
one-way	เที่ยวเดียว	têe·o dee·o
return	ไปกลับ	ƀai glàp
student's	สำหรับนักศึกษา	săm-ràp nák sèuk-săh

| Do I need to book? | ต้องจองล่วงหน้าหรือเปล่า
đôrng jorng lôo·ang nâh rĕu
ƀlòw |
| What time should I check in? | จะต้องมากี่โมง
jà đôrng mah gèe mohng |

PHRASE BUILDER

I'd like a/an ... seat.	ต้องการที่นั่ง ...	đôrng gahn têe nâng ...
aisle	ติดทางเดิน	đìt tahng deun
nonsmoking	ในเขตห้ามสูบบุหรี่	nai kèt hâhm sòop bù·rèe
window	ติดหน้าต่าง	đìt nâh đàhng

Luggage

I'd like a luggage locker.	ต้องการตู้เก็บสัมภาระ đôrng gahn đôo gèp săm-pah-rá
Can I have some coins/ tokens?	ขอเหรียญหน่อย kŏr rĕe·an nòy

PHRASE BUILDER

My luggage has been ...	กระเป๋าของ ผม/ดิฉันโดน ... แล้ว	grà-ɓŏw kŏrng pŏm/dì-chăn dohn ... láa·ou m/f
damaged	เสียหาย	sĕe·a hăi
lost	หายไป	hăi ɓai
stolen	ขโมย	kà-moy

Bus & Train

I'd like to get off at (Saraburi).	ขอลงที่ (สระบุรี) ครับ/ค่ะ kŏr long têe (sà-rà-ɓù-ree) kráp/kâ m/f

29

Excuse me, is this seat free?	ขอโทษ ครับ/ค่ะ ที่นั่งนี้ว่างไหม kŏr tôht kráp/kâ têe nâng née wâhng măi m/f
That's my seat.	นั่นที่นั่งของ ผม/ดิฉัน nân têe nâng kŏng pŏm/ dì-chăn m/f
Please tell me when we get to (Chiang Mai).	เมื่อถึง (เชียงใหม่) กรุณาบอกด้วย mêu·a tĕung (chee·ang mài) gà-rú-nah bòrk dôo·ay
Where's the bus stop?	ที่จอดรถเมล์อยู่ที่ไหน têe jòrt rót mair yòo têe năi
Which bus/songthaew goes to (Ayuthaya)?	รถเมล์/สองแถว คันไหนไป (อยุธยา) rót mair/sŏrng-tăe·ou kan năi ƀai (à-yút-tá-yah)

PHRASE BUILDER

Is this the ... to (Chiang Mai)?	อันนี้เป็น ... ไป (เชียงใหม่) ใช่ไหม	an née ƀen ... ƀai (chee·ang mài) châi măi
boat	เรือ	reu·a
bus	รถเมล	rót mair
train	รถไฟ	rót fai

What station is this?	ที่นี้สถานีไหน têe née sà-tăh-nee năi
What's the next station?	สถานีต่อไปคือสถานีไหน sà-tăh-nee đòr ƀai keu sà- tăh-nee năi

Fast Talk

Taxi, samlor & túk-túk

A fun way to travel short distances in Thailand is by *samlor* (săhm lór สามล้อ) which are three-wheeled bicycle-rickshaws powered by an energetic chauffeur. In city districts that are too congested or chaotic for a săhm lór get a ride with a morđeu-sai ráp jâhng มอเตอร์ไซค์รับจ้าง or motorcyle taxi. Almost emblematic of Thailand's cities is the *túk-túk* (đúk đúk ตุ๊กๆ), a name suggestive of the sound these three-wheeled taxis make as they buzz through the traffic. Bargain hard for all of these transport options, but be sure to offer a tip to any *samlor* driver who works up a worthy sweat.

Does it stop at (Kaeng Koi)?	จอดอยู่ที่ (แก่งคอย) ไหม	jòrt yòo têe (gàang koy) măi
Do I need to change?	ต้องเปลี่ยนรถไหม	dôrng plèe·an rót măi
How many stops to (the museum)?	จอดกี่ป้ายจึงจะถึง (พิพิธภัณฑ์)	jòrt gèe bâi jeung jà těung (pí-pít-tá-pan)

Taxi

Where's the taxi stand?	ที่ขึ้นรถแท็กซี่อยู่ที่ไหน	têe kêun rót táak-sêe yòo têe năi

PHRASE BUILDER

I'd like a taxi ...	ต้องการรถแท็กซี่ ...	dôrng gahn rót-táak sêe ...
at (9am)	เมื่อ (สามโมงเช้า)	mêu·a (săhm mohng chów)
tomorrow	พรุ่งนี้	prûng née

31

PHRASE BUILDER

Please ...	ขอ ...	kŏr ...
slow down	ให้ช้าลง	hâi cháh long
stop here	หยุดตรงนี้	yùt drong née
wait here	คอยอยู่ที่นี่	koy yòo têe née

Is this ... free?	... อันนี้ฟรีหรือเปล่า ... an née free rĕu blòw
How much is it to ...?	ไป ... เท่าไร pai ... tôw-rai
Please take me to (this address).	ขอพาไป (ที่นี่) kŏr pah bai (têe née)
Please put the meter on.	ขอเปิดมิเตอร์ด้วย kŏr bèut mí-đeu dôo·ay

Local Knowledge

Body Language

In Thailand it's important to be aware of your body. Close physical proximity, except in special circumstances such as a crowded Bangkok bus, can be discomforting to Thai people. Thus, you should avoid standing over people or encroaching too much on their personal space.

The head is considered the most sacred part of the body, while the feet are seen as vulgar. Never point at things with your feet nor intentionally touch another person with your feet. Neither should you sit with your feet pointing at someone or at an object of worship, such as a shrine, a picture of the king or Buddha statue. Equally, you should never touch or reach over another person's head. If it's necessary to reach over someone, such as when getting something from a luggage compartment on a bus or train, it's customary to say kŏr tôht ขอโทษ ('Excuse me') first.

Car & Motorbike

I'd like to hire a car.	อยากจะเช่ารถเก๋ง	yàhk jà chôw rót gěng
I'd like to hire a motorbike.	อยากจะเช่ารถมอเตอร์ไซค์	yàhk jà chôw rót mor-đeu-sai
Is this the road to (Ban Bung Wai)?	ทางนี้ไป (บ้านบุ่งหวาย) ไหม	tahng née ɓai (bâhn bùng wăi) măi
Can I park here?	จอดที่นี่ได้ไหม	jòrt têe née dâi măi
Where's a petrol station?	ปั๊มน้ำมันอยู่ที่ไหน	ɓâm nám man yòo têe năi

PHRASE BUILDER

How much for ... hire?	ค่าเช่า ... ละเท่าไร	kâh chôw ... lá tôw-rai
hourly	ชั่วโมง	chôo·a mohng
daily	วัน	wan
weekly	อาทิตย์	ah-tít

Cycling

I'd like to hire a bicycle	ต้องการ เช่ารถจักรยาน	dôrng gahn chôw rót jàk-gà-yahn

Accommodation

⟹ Fast Phrases

I have a reservation.	จองห้องมาแล้ว jorng hôrng mah láa·ou
When is breakfast served?	อาหารเช้าจัด กี่โมง ah-hǎhn chów jàt gèe mohng
What time is checkout?	ต้องออกห้อง กี่โมง đôrng òrk hôrng gèe mohng

Finding Accommodation

PHRASE BUILDER

Where's a ...?	... อยู่ที่ไหน	... yòo têe nǎi
camping ground	ค่ายพักแรม	kâi pák raam
beach hut	กระท่อมชายหาด	grà-tôrm chai hàht
guesthouse	บ้านพัก	bâhn pák
hotel	โรงแรม	rohng raam
temple lodge	วัด	wát
youth hostel	บ้านเยาวชน	bâhn yow-wá-chon

🔊 : LISTEN FOR

| มีห้องว่าง | mee hôrng wâhng | **vacancy** |
| ไม่มีห้องว่าง | mâi mee hôrng wâhng | **no vacancy** |

Booking & Checking In

I have a reservation.	จองห้องมาแล้ว jorng hôrng mah láa·ou

PHRASE BUILDER

Do you have a/an ... room?	มีห้อง ... ไหม	mee hôrng ... mǎi
double	เตียงคู่	đee·ang kôo
single	เดี่ยว	dèe·o
twin	สองเตียง	sǒrng đee·ang

For (three) nights/ weeks.	เป็นเวลา(สาม) คืน/อาทิตย์ ben wair·lah (sǎhm) keun/ah-tít
From ... to	จากวันที่...ถึงวันที่... jàhk wan têe ... těung wan têe ...

PHRASE BUILDER

How much is it per ...?	... ละเท่าไร	... lá tôw-rai
night	คืน	keun
person	คน	kon
week	อาทิตย์	ah-tít

Local Knowledge Hotels

Can you recommend somewhere cheap?	แนะนำที่ราคาถูกได้ไหม náa nam têe rah-kah tòok dâi măi
Can you recommend somewhere nearby?	แนะนำที่ใกล้ ๆ ได้ไหม náa nam têe glâi glâi dâi măi
Can you recommend somewhere romantic?	แนะนำที่โรแมนติกได้ไหม náa nam têe roh-maan-đìk dâi măi

Does the price include breakfast?	ราคาห้องรวมค่าอาหารเช้าด้วยไหม rah-kâh hôrng roo·am kâh ah-hăhn chów dôo·ay măi
Do I need to pay upfront?	ต้องจ่ายเงินล่วงหน้าไหม đôrng jài ngeun lôo·ang nâh măi
Can I see it?	ดูได้ไหม doo dâi măi
I'll take it.	เอา ow

Requests & Questions

When is breakfast served?	อาหารเช้าจัดกี่โมง ah-hăhn chów jàt gèe mohng

PHRASE BUILDER

Can I use the ...?	ใช้ ... ได้ไหม	chái ... dâi măi
kitchen	ห้องครัว	hôrng kroo·a
laundry	ห้องซักผ้า	hôrng sák pâh
telephone	โทรศัพท์	toh-rá-sàp

Where is breakfast served?	อาหารเช้าจัดที่ไหน ah-hǎhn chów jàt têe nǎi
Please wake me at (seven).	กรุณาปลุกให้เวลา (เจ็ด) นาฬิกา gà-rú-nah blùk hâi wair-lah (jèt) nah-lí-gah
Could I have the key, please?	ขอกุญแจห้องหน่อย kǒr gun-jaa hôrng nòy
Can I get another (blanket)?	ขอ (ผ้าห่ม) อีกผืนได้ไหม kǒr (pâh hòm) èek pěun dâi mǎi

---

PHRASE BUILDER
....

Do you have a/ an ...?	มี ... ไหม	mee ... mǎi
elevator	ลิฟท์	líp
laundry service	บริการซักผ้า	bor-rí-gahn sák pâh
safe	ตู้เซฟ	ɖôo sép

Do you arrange tours here?	ที่นี่จัดนำเที่ยวไหม têe née jàt nam têe·o mǎi
Do you change money here?	ที่นี่แลกเงินได้ไหม têe née lâak ngeun dâi mǎi

Complaints

There's no hot water.	ไม่มีน้ำร้อน mâi mee nám rórn
The air-conditioning doesn't work.	แอร์ เสีย aa sěe·a

Fast Talk

Using Patterns

Look out for patterns of words or phrases that stay the same, even when the situation changes, eg 'Do you have ...?' or 'I'd like to ...'. If you can recognise these patterns, you're already halfway there to creating a full phrase. The dictionary will help you put other words together with these patterns to convey your meaning – even if it's not completely grammatically correct in all contexts, the dictionary form will always be understood.

The fan doesn't work.	พัดลม เสีย pát lom sĕe·a
The toilet doesn't work.	ส้วม เสีย sôo·am sĕe·a
This (pillow) isn't clean.	(หมอนใบ) นี้ไม่สะอาด (mŏrn bai) née mâi sà·àht

PHRASE BUILDER

It's too ...	... เกินไป	... geun bai
cold	หนาว	nŏw
dark	มืด	mêut
noisy	เสียงดัง	sĕe·ang dang
small	เล็ก	lék

Checking Out

What time is checkout?	ต้องออกจากห้องกี่โมง dôrng òrk jàhk hôrng gèe mohng

PHRASE BUILDER

Could I have my ..., please?	ขอ ... หน่อย	kŏr ... nòy
deposit	เงินมัดจำ	ngeun mát jam
passport	หนังสือเดินทาง	năng-sĕu deun tahng
valuables	ของมีค่า	kŏrng mee kâh

Can I leave my bags here?	ฝากกระเป๋าไว้ที่นี่ได้ไหม fàhk grà-Ďŏw wái têe née dâi măi

Eating & Drinking

Fast Phrases

I'd like the menu , please.	ขอรายการอาหารหน่อย kŏr rai gahn ah-hǎhn nòy
I'd like (a beer), please.	ขอเบียร์หน่อย kŏr bee·a nòy
Please bring the bill.	ขอบิลล์หน่อย kŏr bin nòy

Meals

breakfast	อาหารเช้า ah-hǎhn chów
lunch	อาหารกลางวัน ah-hǎhn glahng wan
dinner	อาหารเย็น ah-hǎhn yen
snack	อาหารว่าง ah-hǎhn wâhng
eat (informal)	กิน gin
eat (polite)	ทาน tahn

Fast Talk

Have You Eaten Yet?

The cultural importance of food in Thailand can hardly be underestimated. In fact, a common Thai pleasantary is gin kôw rĕu yang กินข้าวหรือยัง which means 'Have you eaten yet?'. How you choose to answer is not so important – this greeting is really just a way of affirming a friendly connection.

eat (very formal)	รับประทาน ráp Þrà-tahn
drink	เครื่องดื่ม krêu·ang dèum

Finding a Place to Eat

Where would you go for a cheap meal?	ถ้าคุณจะไปหาอาหารราคาถูกๆคุณจะ ไปไหน tâh kun jà Þai hăh ah-hăhn rah-kah tòok tòok kun jà Þai năi
Where would you go for local specialities?	ถ้าคุณจะไปหาอาหารรส เด็ดๆของแถวนี้คุณจะไปไหน tâh kun jà Þai hăh ah-hăhn rót dèt dèt kŏrng tăa·ou née kun jà Þai năi

PHRASE BUILDER

Can you recommend a ...	แนะนำ... ได้ไหม	náa-nam ... dâi măi
bar	บาร์	bah
café	ร้านกาแฟ	ráhn gah-faa
restaurant	ร้านอาหาร	ráhn ah-hăhn

41

Fast Talk

Practising Thai

If you want to practise your language skills, try the waiters at a restaurant. Find your feet with straight-forward phrases such as asking for a table and ordering a drink, then initiate a conversation by asking for menu recommendations or asking how a dish is cooked. And as you'll often know food terms even before you've 'officially' learnt a word of the language, you're already halfway to understanding the response.

Are you still serving food?	ยังบริการอาหารไหม yang bor-rí-gahn ah-hăhn măi
How long is the wait?	ต้องรอนานเท่าไร dôrng ror nahn tôw-rai
I'd like to reserve a table for (two) people	ผม/ดิฉันอยากจะจองโต๊ะสำหรับ (สอง) คน pŏm/dì-chăn yàhk jà jorng đó săm-ràp (sŏrng) kon m/f
I'd like to reserve a table for (eight pm)	ผม/ดิฉันอยากจะจองโต๊ะสำหรับ เวลา(สองทุ่ม) pŏm/dì-chăn yàhk jà jorng đó săm-ràp wair-lah (sŏrng tûm) m/f

PHRASE BUILDER

I'd like ..., please.	ขอ...หน่อย	kŏr ... nòy
a table for (five)	โต๊ะสำหรับ(ห้า) คน	đó săm-ràp (hâh) kon
nonsmoking	ที่เขตห้ามสูบบุหรี่	têe kèt hâhm sòop bù-rèe

Ordering & Paying

What would you recommend?	คุณแนะนำอะไรบ้าง kun náa-nam à-rai bâhng
What's the local speciality?	อาหารรสเด็ดๆ ของแถวนี้คืออะไร ah-hǎhn rót dèt dèt kǒrng tǎe·ou née keu à-rai
I'd like it with ...	ต้องการแบบมี ... dôrng gahn bàap mee ...
I'd like it without ...	ต้องการแบบไม่มี ... dôrng gahn bàap mâi mee ...
This is (too) cold	อันนี้เย็น (เกินไป) an née yen (geun bai)
That was delicious!	อร่อยมาก à-ròy mâhk
Please bring the bill.	ขอบิลล์หน่อย kǒr bin nòy
Please bring a (wine) glass.	ขอแก้ว(ไวน์) หน่อย kǒr gâe·ou (wai) nòy

PHRASE BUILDER

Could you prepare a meal without ...?	ทำอาหารไม่ใส่ ... ได้ไหม	tam ah-hǎhn mâi sài ... dâi mǎi
butter	เนย	neu·i
eggs	ไข่	kài
fish	ปลา	blah
meat stock	ซุปก้อนเนื้อ	súp gôrn néu·a
pork	เนื้อหมู	néu·a mǒo
poultry	เนื้อไก่	néu·a gài

PHRASE BUILDER

I'd like it ...	ต้องการ ...	đôrng gahn ...
medium	ปานกลาง	bahn glahng
rare	ไม่สุกมาก	mâi sùk mâhk
steamed	นึ่ง	nêung
well-done	สุกมากหน่อย	sùk mâhk nòy

I'd like the drink list, please.	ขอรายการเครื่องดื่มหน่อย kŏr rai gahn krêu·ang dèum nòy
I'd like the menu, please.	ขอรายการอาหารหน่อย kŏr rai gahn ah-hăhn nòy

Special Diets & Allergies

I'm (a) vegan.	ผม/ดิฉัน ไม่ทานอาหารที่มาจากสัตว์ pŏm/dì-chăn mâi tahn ah-hăhn têe mah jàhk sàt m/f
I'm (a) vegetarian.	ผม/ดิฉัน ทานอาหารเจ pŏm/dì-chăn tahn ah-hăhn jair m/f

PHRASE BUILDER

I'm allergic to ...	ผม/ดิฉันแพ้ ...	pŏm/dì-chăn páa ...
dairy produce	อาหารจำพวกนม	ah-hăhn jam-pôo·ak nom
gluten	แป้ง	bâang
MSG	ชูรส	choo-rót
nuts	ถั่ว	tòo·a
seafood	อาหารทะเล	ah-hăhn tá-lair
shellfish	หอย	hŏy

Non-alcoholic Drinks

(cup of) coffee	กาแฟ(ถ้วยหนึ่ง) gah-faa (tôo·ay nèung)
(cup of) tea	ชา(ถ้วยหนึ่ง) chah (tôo·ay nèung)
... with milk	...ใส่นม ... sài nom
... without	...ไม่ใส่ ... mâi sài
sugar	น้ำตาล nám-đahn
orange juice	น้ำส้มคั้น nám sôm kán
soft drink	น้ำอัดลม nám àt lom
mineral water	น้ำแร่ nám râa

PHRASE BUILDER

a ... of beer	เบียร์...หนึ่ง	bee·a ... nèung
glass	แก้ว	gâa·ou
jug	เหยือก	yèu·ak
pint	ไพนต์	pai

Alcoholic Drinks

beer	เบียร์ bee·a

brandy	บรั่นดี
	bà-ràn-dee
cocktail	ค็อกเทล
	kórk-ten
a shot of whisky	วิสกี้ช็อตหนึ่ง
	wít-sà-gêe chórt nèung
Cheers!	ไชโย
	chai-yoh

PHRASE BUILDER

a glass/bottle of ... wine	ไวน์...แก้วหนึ่ง/ ขวดหนึ่ง	wai ... gâa·ou nèung/kòo·at nèung
red	แดง	daang
white	ขาว	kŏw

In the Bar

I'll buy you a drink.	ฉันจะซื้อของดื่มให้คุณ
	chăn jà séu kŏrng dèum hâi kun
What would you like?	จะรับอะไร
	jà ráp à-rai
I'll have ...	จะเอา ...
	jà ow ...
Same again, please.	ขออีกครั้งหนึ่ง
	kŏr èek kráng nèung
It's my round.	ตาของฉันนะ
	đah kŏrng chăn ná

Garçon

When calling for the attention of a waiter or waitress, make sure you use the correct form of address. A waiter is called bǒy บ๋อย which is easy enough to remember – just think of the English word 'boy' and raise the tone as if you are asking a question.

Buying Food

How much is (a kilo of mangoes)?	(มะม่วงกิโลหนึ่ง) เท่าไร	(má-môo·ang gì-loh nèung) tôw-rai
What's that?	นั่นคืออะไร	nân keu à-rai
How much?	เท่าไร	tôw-rai
Can I taste it?	ชิมได้ไหม	chím dâi mǎi
A bit more.	มากขึ้นหน่อย	mâhk kêun nòy
Enough!	พอแล้ว	por láa·ou

PHRASE BUILDER

I'd like ...	ต้องการ ...	đôrng gahn ...
(200) grams	(สองร้อย) กรัม	(sǒrng róy) gram
(three) pieces	(สาม) ชิ้น	(sǎhm) chín
that one	อันนั้น	an nán

Menu Decoder

b

bai đeu·i ใบเตย *pandanus leaves –
used primarily to add a vanilla-like flavour
to Thai sweets*

bai đorng ใบตอง *banana leaves*

bai gà·prow ใบกะเพรา *'holy basil' –
so-called due to its sacred status in India*

bai maang·lák ใบแมงลัก *known
variously as Thai basil, lemon basil or mint
basil – popular in soups & as a condiment
for* kà·nŏm jeen nám yah & *lâhp*

bai má·gròot ใบมะกรูด *kaffir lime
leaves*

bà·mèe บะหมี่ *yellowish noodles made
from wheat flour & sometimes egg*

bà·mèe gée·o boo บะหมี่เกี๊ยวปู
soup containing bà·mèe, *won ton &
crab meat*

bà·mèe hâang บะหมี่แห้ง *bà·mèe
served in a bowl with a little garlic oil,
meat, seafood or vegetables*

bà·mèe nám บะหมี่น้ำ *bà·mèe with
broth, meat, seafood or vegetables*

bòo·ap บวบ *gourd*

bòo·ap lèe·am บวบเหลี่ยม *sponge
gourd*

bòo·ap ngoo บวบงู *snake gourd*

b

bah·tôrng·gŏh ปาท่องโก๋ *fried
wheat pastry similar to an unsweetened
doughnut*

bèt เป็ด *duck*

bèt yâhng เป็ดย่าง *roast duck*

blah ปลา *fish*

blah bèuk ปลาบึก *giant Mekong
catfish*

blah chôrn ปลาช่อน *serpent-headed
fish – a freshwater variety*

blah dàak ปลาแดก *see* blah·ráh

blah dàat dee·o ปลาแดดเดียว *'half-
day dried fish' – fried & served with a spicy
mango salad*

blah dùk ปลาดุก *catfish*

blah gà·dàk ปลากะตัก *type of an-
chovy used in* nám blah *(fish sauce)*

blah gà·pong ปลากะพง *seabass •
ocean perch*

blah gŏw ปลาเก๋า *grouper • reef cod*

blah grà·bòrk ปลากระบอก *mullet*

blah kem ปลาเค็ม *preserved salted fish*

blah lăi ปลาไหล *freshwater eel*

blah lòt ปลาหลด *saltwater eel*

blah mèuk glôo·ay ปลาหมึกกล้วย
squid • calamari

blah mèuk grà·dorng ปลาหมึก
กระดอง *cuttlefish*

blah nin ปลานิล *tilapia (variety of fish)*

blah pŏw ปลาเผา *fish wrapped in
banana leaves or foil & roasted over (or
covered in) hot coals*

blah sah·deen ปลาซาร์ดีน *sardine*

blah săm·lee ปลาสำลี *cottonfish*

blah săm·lee pŏw ปลาสำลีเผา *'fire-*

roasted cottonfish' – cottonfish roasted
over coals
ѣlah too ปลาทู *mackerel*
ѣlah tôrt ปลาทอด *fried fish*
ѣlah-ráh ปลาร้า *'rotten fish' –
unpasteurised version of* nám ѣlah *sold in
earthenware jars (North-East Thailand)*
ѣó ɖàak โป๊ะแตก *'broken fish trap
soup' –* ɖôm yam *with the addition of
either sweet or holy basil & a melange of
seafood, usually including squid, crab, fish,
mussels & shrimp*
ѣoo ปู *crab*
ѣoo nah ปูนา *field crabs*
ѣor-ѣée·a ปอเปี๊ยะ *egg rolls*
ѣor-ѣée·a sòt ปอเปี๊ยะสด *fresh
spring rolls*
ѣor-ѣée·a tôrt ปอเปี๊ยะทอด *fried
spring rolls*

ɖ

ɖaang moh แตงโม *watermelon*
ɖà-krái ตะไคร้ *lemongrass – used in
curry pastes,* tôm yam, yam *& certain
kinds of* lâhp
ɖôm kàh gài ต้มข่าไก่ *'boiled galangal
chicken' – includes lime, chilli & coconut
milk (Central Thailand)*
ɖôm yam gûng ต้มยำกุ้ง *shrimp* yam
ɖôm yam ѣó ɖàak ต้มยำโป๊ะแตก
ɖôm yam *with mixed seafood*
ɖôn hörm ต้นหอม *'fragrant plant' –
spring onion or scallions*
ɖôw hôo เต้าหู้ *tofu (soybean curd)*

---

f

fák ฟัก *gourd • squash*
fák kěe·o ฟักเขียว *wax gourd*
fák torng ฟักทอง *golden squash or
Thai pumpkin*
fà-ràng ฝรั่ง *guava (the word also refers
to a Westerner of European descent)*

---

g

gaang แกง *classic chilli-based curries
for which Thai cuisine is famous, as well
as any dish with a lot of liquid (thus it can
refer to soups)*
gaang ѣàh แกงป่า *'forest curry' – spicy
curry which uses no coconut milk*
gaang ɖai ѣlah แกงไตปลา *curry
made with fish stomach, green beans,
pickled bamboo shoots & potatoes (South
Thailand)*
gaang gah-yöo แกงกาหยู *curry made
with fresh cashews – popular in Phuket
& Ranong*
gaang gà-rèe gài แกงกะหรี่ไก่ *curry
similar to an Indian curry, containing
potatoes & chicken*
gaang hó แกงโฮะ *spicy soup featuring
pickled bamboo shoots (North Thailand)*
gaang jèut wún sên แกงจืดวุ้นเส้น
mung bean noodle soup, gaang jèut *with*
wún-sên
gaang kà-nŭn แกงขนุน *jackfruit curry
– favoured in Northern Thailand but found
elsewhere as well*
gaang kěe·o wähn แกงเขียวหวาน
green curry
gaang gôo·a sôm sàp-ѣà-rót
แกงคั่วส้มสับปะรด *pan-roasted
pineapple curry with sea crab*
gaang lee·ang แกงเลียง *spicy soup of
green or black peppercorns, sponge gourd,
baby corn, cauliflower & various greens,
substantiated with pieces of chicken,
shrimp or ground pork – probably one of
the oldest recipes in Thailand*
gaang lěu·ang แกงเหลือง *'yellow
curry' – spicy dish of fish cooked with green
squash, pineapple, green beans & green
papaya (South Thailand)*
gaang morn แกงมอญ *Mon curry*
gaang pèt แกงเผ็ด *red curry*
gaang ɖäht kôw แกงราดข้าว *curry
over rice*

gaang sôm แกงส้ม *soupy, salty, sweet & sour curry made with dried chillies, shallots, garlic & Chinese key (grà-chai) pestled with salt, gà-bì & fish sauce*

gah-lǎh กาหลา *'torch ginger' – thinly-sliced flower buds from a wild ginger plant, sometimes used in the Southern Thai rice salad kòw yam*

gài ไก่ *chicken*

gài tôrt ไก่ทอด *fried chicken*

gà-bì กะปิ *shrimp paste*

gàp glàam กับแกล้ม *'drinking food' – dishes specifically meant to be eaten while drinking alcoholic beverages*

gà-rèe กะหรี่ *Thai equivalent of the Anglo-Indian term 'curry'*

gà-tí กะทิ *coconut milk*

gée-o เกี๊ยว *won ton – triangle of dough wrapped around ground pork or fish*

glâh กล้า *rice sprouts*

glôo-ay กล้วย *banana*

goh-bée โกปี๊ *Hokkien dialect for coffee, used especially in Trang province*

goh-bée dam โกปี๊ดำ *sweetened black coffee (Trang province)*

goh-bée dam mâi sài nám-dahn โกปี๊ดำไม่ใส่น้ำตาล *unsweetened black coffee (Trang province)*

gǒo-ay đěe-o ก๋วยเตี๋ยว *rice noodles made from pure rice flour mixed with water to form a paste which is then steamed to form wide, flat sheets*

gǒo-ay đěe-o hâang ก๋วยเตี๋ยวแห้ง *dry rice noodles*

gǒo-ay đěe-o hâang sù-kŏh-tai ก๋วยเตี๋ยวแห้งสุโขทัย *'Sukothai dry rice noodles' – thin rice noodles served in a bowl with peanuts, barbecued pork, ground dried chilli, green beans & bean sprouts*

gǒo-ay đěe-o jan-tá-bù-ree ก๋วยเตี๋ยวจันทบุรี *dried rice noodles (Chantaburi)*

gǒo-ay đěe-o lôok chín blah ก๋วยเตี๋ยวลูกชิ้นปลา *rice noodles with fish balls*

gǒo-ay đěe-o reu-a ก๋วยเตี๋ยวเรือ *'boat noodles' – concoction of dark beef broth & rice noodles originally sold only on boats that frequented the canals of Rangsit*

gǒo-ay jáp ก๋วยจั๊บ *thick broth of sliced Chinese mushrooms & bits of chicken or pork*

gôy ก้อย *raw spicy minced-meat salad*

gûng gù-lah dam กุ้งกุลาดำ *tiger prawn*

gûng mang-gorn กุ้งมังกร *'dragon prawn' – refers to lobster*

gûng súp bâang tôrt กุ้งชุบแป้งทอด *batter-fried shrimp*

h

hǎng gà-tí หางกะทิ *coconut milk*

hèt hŏrm เห็ดหอม *shiitake mushrooms*

hŏm daang หอมแดง *shallots • scallions*

hǒo-a chai tów หัวไชเท้า *Chinese radish*

hǒo-a gà-tí หัวกะทิ *coconut cream*

hǒo-a pàk gàht หัวผักกาด *giant white radish*

hòr mòk tá-lair ห่อหมกทะเล *hòr hǒy* หอย *clams & oysters (generic)*

hǒy kraang หอยแครง *cockle*

hǒy má-laang pôo หอยแมลงภู่ *green mussel*

hǒy nahng rom หอยนางรม *oyster*

hǒy pát หอยพัด *scallop*

j

jàa-ou hórn แจ่วฮ้อน *North-Eastern version of Central Thailand's popular Thai sukiyaki (sù-gêe-yah-gêe) but includes mung bean noodles, thin-sliced beef, beef entrails, egg, water spinach, cabbage & cherry tomatoes*

jóhk โจ๊ก *thick rice soup or congee*

jóhk gài โจ๊กไก่ *thick rice soup with chicken*

jóhk mŏo โจ๊กหมู thick rice soup with pork meatballs

k

kàh ข่า galangal (also known as Thai ginger)

kài ไข่ egg

kài ปิ๊ง ไข่ปิ้ง eggs in their shells skewered on a sharp piece of bamboo & grilled over hot coals

kài pӑm ไข่ผ่ำ small green plant that grows on the surface of ponds, bogs & other still waters (North-East Thailand)

kài pàt hèt hŏo nŏo ไข่ผัดเห็ดหูหนู eggs stir-fried with mouse-ear mushrooms

kà-mîn ขมิ้น turmeric

kà-nŏm ขนม Thai sweets

kà-nŏm jeen ขนมจีน 'Chinese Pastry' – rice noodles produced by pushing rice-flour paste through a sieve into boiling water – served on a plate & mixed with various curries

kà-nŏm jeen chow nám ขนมจีนชาวน้ำ noodle dish featuring a mixture of pineapple, coconut, dried shrimp, ginger & garlic served with kà-nŏm jeen

kà-nŏm jeen tôrt man ขนมจีนทอด มัน thin rice noodles with fried fish cake from Phetchaburi

kà-nŏm jèep ขนมจีบ Chinese dumplings filled with shrimp or pork

kà-nŭn ขนุน jackfruit (also known as màhk mêe in Isaan dialect)

kǐng ขิง ginger

kŏrng wăhn ของหวาน sweets

kôw ข้าว rice

kôw ปล่òw ข้าวเปล่า plain rice

kôw bow ข้าวเบา 'light rice' – early season rice

kôw dôm ข้าวต้ม boiled rice soup, a popular late-night meal

kôw gaang ข้าวแกง curry over rice

kôw glahng ข้าวกลาง 'middle rice' – rice that matures mid-season

kôw glàm ข้าวก่ำ type of sticky rice with a deep purple, almost black hue, for use in desserts and, in Northern Thailand, to produce a mild home-made rice wine of the same name

kôw glôrng ข้าวกล้อง brown rice

kôw grèe·ap gûng ข้าวเกรียบกุ้ง shrimp chips

kôw hŏrm má-lí ข้าวหอม มะลิ jasmine rice

kôw jòw ข้าวเจ้า white rice

kôw kôo·a ปòn ข้าวคั่วปน uncooked rice dry-roasted in a pan till it begins to brown, then pulverised with a mortar & pestle – one of the most important ingredients in lâhp

kôw lăhm ข้าวหลาม sticky rice & coconut steamed in a bamboo joint, a Nakhon Pathom speciality

kôw man gài ข้าวมันไก่ Hainanese dish of sliced steamed chicken over rice cooked in chicken broth & garlic

kôw nĕe·o ข้าวเหนียว sticky rice that is popular in Northern & North-Eastern Thailand

kôw pàt ข้าวผัด fried rice

kôw pàt năam ข้าวผัดแหนม fried rice with năam

kôw pôht ข้าวโพด corn

kôw pôht òrn ข้าวโพดอ่อน baby corn

kôw râi ข้าวไร่ plantation rice or mountain rice

kôw sŏo·ay ข้าวสวย cooked rice

krêu·ang gaang เครื่องแกง curry paste created by mashing, pounding & grinding an array of ingredients with a stone mortar & pestle to form an aromatic, thick & very pungent-tasting paste (also known as nám prík gaang)

krêu·ang gaang pèt เครื่องแกงเผ็ด red krêu·ang gaang made with dried red chillies

51

l

lahng sàht ลางสาด oval-shaped fruit with white fragrant flesh, grown in Utaradit Province

lâhp bèt ลาบเป็ด duck lâhp, an Ubon Ratchathani speciality

lâhp bèt daang ลาบเป็ดแดง red duck lâhp which uses duck blood as part of the sauce

lâhp bèt kŏw ลาบเป็ดขาว white duck lâhp

lâhp sùk ลาบสุก cooked lâhp

lam yai ลำใย longan fruit (also known as 'dragon's eyes')

lá-mút ละมุด sapodilla fruit

lôhk chín ลูกชิ้นปลา fish balls

lôhk grà-wahn ลูกกระวาน cardamom

m

má-gròot มะกรูด kaffir lime – small citrus fruit with a bumpy & wrinkled skin

má-kăhm มะขาม tamarind

má-kĕu·a มะเขือ eggplant • aubergine

má-kĕu·a bròo มะเขือเปราะ Thai eggplant – popular curry ingredient

má-kĕu·a poo·ang มะเขือพวง 'pea eggplant' – popular curry ingredient, especially for gaang kĕe·o·wăhn

má-kĕu·a têt มะเขือเทศ tomatoes

má-lá-gor มะละกอ paw paw • papaya

má-môo·ang มะม่วง mango

man fà-ràng มันฝรั่ง potato

man fà-ràng tôrt มันฝรั่งทอด fried potatoes

man gâa·ou มันแกว yam root • jicama

má-now มะนาว lime

má-prów มะพร้าว coconut

má-prow òrn มะพร้าวอ่อน young green coconut

mét má-môo·ang hĭm-má-pahn tôrt เม็ดมะม่วงหิมพานต์ทอด fried cashew nuts

mŏo หมู pork

mŏo bîng หมูปิ้ง toasted pork

mŏo daang หมูแดง strips of bright red barbecued pork

mŏo săhm chán หมูสามชั้น 'three level pork' – cuts that include meat, fat & skin

mŏo sàp หมูสับ ground pork

mŏo yor หมูยอ sausage resembling a large German frankfurter

n

năam แหนม pickled pork

năam môr แหนมหม้อ 'pot sausage' – sausage made of ground pork, pork rind & cooked sticky rice & fermented in a clay pot with salt, garlic & chilli (North Thailand)

nòr mái หน่อไม้ bamboo shoots

nòr mái brêe·o หน่อไม้เปรี้ยว pickled bamboo shoots

nám blah น้ำปลา fish sauce – thin, clear, amber sauce made from fermented anchovies & used to season Thai dishes

nám dow น้ำเต้า bottle gourd

nám jîm น้ำจิ้ม dipping sauces

nám jîm ah-hăhn tá-lair น้ำจิ้ม อาหารทะเล seafood dipping sauce, prík nám blah with the addition of minced garlic, lime juice & sugar

nám prík dah daang น้ำพริกตาแดง 'red eye chilli dip' – very dry & hot dip

nám prík gaang น้ำพริกแกง see krêu·ang gaang

nám prík gà·bì น้ำพริกกะปิ nám prík made with shrimp paste & fresh prík kêe

nám see-éw น้ำซีอิ๊ว soy sauce

nám sôm prík น้ำส้มพริก sliced green chillies in vinegar

nám yah น้ำยา standard curry topping for kà-nŏm jeen, made of Chinese key (gra-chai) & ground or pounded fish

nám-dahn běep น้ำตาลปีบ soft, light palm sugar paste – the most raw form of palm sugar

néu·a เนื้อ beef

néu·a nám dòk เนื้อน้ำตก *'waterfall beef'* – sliced barbecued beef in a savoury dressing of lime juice, ground chilli & other seasonings

néu·a pàt nám-man hŏy เนื้อผัดน้ำมันหอย beef stir-fried in oyster sauce

p

prík ȯ̀bn พริกป่น *dried red chilli (usually nám prík chée fáh), flaked or ground to a near powder*

prík chée·fáh พริกชี้ฟ้า *'sky-pointing chilli'* – also known as spur chilli, Thai Chilli and Japanese chilli

prík nám ȯ̀lah พริกน้ำปลา *standard condiment of sliced fresh red & green* prík kêe nŏo *(chilli) floating in fish sauce*

prík nám sôm พริกนาส้ม *young* prík yòo·ak *pickled in vinegar – a condiment popular with noodle dishes & Chinese food*

prík tai พริกไทย *black pepper (also known in English as Thai pepper)*

prík wăhn พริกหวาน *'sweet pepper'* – green bell pepper

r

râht nâh ราดหน้า *shortened name for any* gŏo·ay-dĕe·o râht nâh *dish, frequently used when ordering*

râht prík ราดพริก prík *smothered in garlic, chillies & onions – usually accompanies freshwater fish*

roh-dee โรตี *fried, round & flat wheat bread descended from the Indian paratha*

roh-dee kài โรตีไข่ *roti cooked with egg*

s

sah-lah-ȯ̀bow ซาลาเปา *steamed buns filled with stewed pork or sweet bean paste*

see-éw dam ซีอิ๊วดำ *'black soy'* – heavy, dark soy sauce

see-éw kŏw ซีอิ๊วขาว *'white soy'* – light soy sauce

sà-dé สะเต๊ะ satay – *short skewers of barbecued beef, pork or chicken that are served with a spicy peanut sauce*

sà-dé mŏo สะเต๊ะหมู *satay pork*

sà-dé néu·a สะเต๊ะเนื้อ *satay beef*

săng-kà-yăh fák torng สังขยาฟักทอง *custard-filled pumpkin*

sàp-ȯ̀à-rót สับปะรด *pineapple*

sà-rá-nàa สะระแหน่ *mint*

sên lék เส้นเล็ก *thick rice noodles*

sên mèe เส้นหมี่ *thin rice noodles*

sên yài เส้นใหญ่ *medium-thick rice noodles*

sôm kĕe·o wăhn ส้มเขียวหวาน *mandarin orange*

sôm oh ส้มโอ *pomelo – popular in Northern Thailand*

t

tòo·a ȯ̀bn ถั่วป่น *ground peanuts*

tòo·a lan-dow ถั่วลันเตา *snow peas*

tòo·a lĕu·ang ถั่วเหลือง *soya bean*

tòo·a ngôrk ถั่วงอก *mung bean sprouts*

tòo·a tôrt ถั่วทอด *fried peanuts*

tôrt man ȯ̀lah ทอดมันปลา *fried fish cake*

tôrt man gûng ทอดมันกุ้ง *fried shrimp cake*

y

yam gài ยำไก่ *hot & tangy salad with chicken & mint*

yam hèt hŏrm ยำเห็ดหอม *hot & tangy salad made with fresh shiitake mushrooms*

yêe-ràh ยี่หร่า *cumin*

Sightseeing

≡ Fast Phrases

When's the museum open?	พิพิธพันธ์ เปิดกี่โมง pí-pít-tá-pan bèut gèe mohng
When's the next tour?	การนำเที่ยวครั้งต่อไปกี่โมง gahn nam têe·o kráng dòr bai gèe mohng
Can we take photos?	ถ่ายรูปได้ไหม tài rôop dâi măi

Planning

Do you have information on local places of interest?	มีข้อมูลเกี่ยวกับแหล่งท่องเที่ยวที่น่าสนใจแถวนี้ไหม mee kôr moon gèe·o gàp laang tôrng têe·o têe nâh sŏn jai tăa·ou née măi
I have (one day).	มีเวลา(หนึ่งวัน) mee wair-lah nèung wan
Can we hire a guide?	จ้างไกด์นำเที่ยวได้ไหม jâhng gai nam têe·o dâi măi
I'd like to see ...	ผม/ดิฉัน อยากจะดู ... pŏm/dì-chăn yàhk jà doo ... m/f

54

PHRASE BUILDER

I'd like ...	ผม/ดิฉัน ต้องการ ...	pŏm/dì-chăn đôrng gahn m/f
an audio set	ชุดเทปนำเที่ยว	chút tép nam têe·o
a catalogue	คู่มือแนะนำ	kôo meu náa nam
a guidebook in English	คู่มือนำเที่ยว เป็นภาษาอังกฤษ	kôo meu nam têe·o ben pah-săh ang-grìt
a (local) map	แผนที่ (ท้องถิ่น)	păan têe (tórng tìn)

Questions

What's that?	นั่นคืออะไร nân keu à-rai
Who made it?	ใครสร้าง krai sâhng
How old is it?	เก่าเท่าไร gòw tôw-rai
Could you take a photo of me?	ถ่ายรูปให้ผม/ดิฉันหน่อยได้ไหม tài rôop hâi pŏm/dì-chăn nòy dâi măi m/f
Can I take a photo (of you)?	ถ่ายรูป (คุณ) ได้ไหม tài rôop (kun) dâi măi
I'll send you the photo.	จะส่งภาพมาให้ jà sòng pâhp ma hâi

Getting In

What time does it open/ close?	เปิด/ปิด กี่โมง bèut/bìt gèe mohng

55

Fast Talk

Forming Sentences

You don't need to memorise complete sentences; instead, simply use key words to get your meaning across. For example, you might know that mêu·a rai เมื่อไร means 'when' in Thai. So if you've arranged a tour but don't know what time, just ask เมื่อไรทัวร์ [mêu·a rai too·a]. Don't worry that you're not getting the whole sentence right – people will understand if you stick to the key words.

What's the admission charge?
ค่าเข้าเท่าไร
kâh kôw tôw-rai

PHRASE BUILDER

Is there a discount for ...?	ลดราคาสำหรับ ... ไหม	lót rah-kah săm-ràp ... măi
children	เด็ก	dèk
families	ครอบครัว	krôrp kroo·a
groups	คณะ	ká-ná
older people	คนสูงอายุ	kon sŏong ah-yú
pensioners	คนกินเงินบำนาญ	kon gin ngeun bam-nahn
students	นักศึกษา	nák sèuk-săh

Galleries & Museums

When's the gallery open?
หอแสดงเปิดกี่โมง
hŏr sà-daang bèut gèe mohng

When's the museum open?	พิพิธพันธ์ เปิดกี่โมง pí-pít-tá-pan bèut gèe mohng
What's in the collection?	มีอะไรบ้างในชุดนี้ mee à-rai bâhng nai chút née
It's a/an exhibition of ...	เป็นนิทรรศการแสดง... ben ní-tát-sà-gahn sà-daang...
I like the works of ...	ผม/ดิฉันชอบงานของ ... pŏm/dì-chăn chôrp ngahn kŏrng ... m/f
... art	ศิลปะ ... sĭn-lá-bà ...
graphic	การเขียน gahn kĕe·an
modern	สมัยใหม่ sà-măi mài
performance	การแสดง gahn sà-daang

Tours

When's the next ...?	... ต่อไปออกกี่โมง ... dòr bai òrk gèe mohng

PHRASE BUILDER

Can you recommend a ...?	แนะนำ ... ได้ไหม	náa-nam ... dâi măi
boat-trip	เที่ยวเรือ	têe·o reu·a
day trip	เที่ยวรายวัน	têe·o rai wan
tour	ทัวร์	too·a

Do I need to take ... with me?	ต้องเอา...ไปด้วยไหม đôrng ow ... bai dôo·ay mǎi
How long is the tour?	การเที่ยวใช้เวลานานเท่าไร gahn têe·o chái wair-lah nahn tôw-rai
What time should we be back?	ควรจะกลับมากี่โมง koo·an jà glàp mah gèe mohng
I've lost my group.	ผม/ดิฉัน หลงคณะอยู่ pǒm/dì-chǎn lǒng ká-ná yòo m/f

PHRASE BUILDER

Is ... included?	รวม ... ด้วยไหม	roo·am ... dôo·ay mǎi
the admission charge	ค่าเข้า	kâh kôw
equipment	อุปกรณ์	ùp-bà-gorn
food	ค่าอาหาร	kâh ah-hǎhn
transport	ค่าการขนส่ง	kâh gahn kǒn sòng

58

Shopping

≡ Fast Phrases

Can I look at?	ขอดูได้ไหม
	kŏr doo dâi măi
How much is it?	ราคาเท่าไร
	rah-kah tôw rai
That's too expensive.	แพงไป
	paang bai

Looking For ...

Where can I buy locally produced goods?	จะซื้อผลิตภัณฑ์ท้องถิ่นได้ที่ไหน
	jà séu pà-lìt-tá-pan tórng tìn dâi têe năi

PHRASE BUILDER

Where's ...?	... อยู่ที่ไหน	... yòo têe năi
a department store	ห้างสรรพสินค้า	hâhng sàp-pá-sĭn-káh
a floating market	ตลาดน้ำ	đà-làht nám
a market	ตลาด	đà-làht
a supermarket	ซูเปอร์มาร์เก็ต	soo-beu-mah-gèt

59

Shops

Where would you go for bargains?	จะซื้อของราคาดีๆได้ที่ไหน jà séu kŏrng rah-kah dee dee dâi têe năi
Where would you go for souvenirs?	จะซื้อของที่ระลึกได้ที่ไหน jà séu kŏrng têe rà-léuk dâi têe năi

Where can I buy locally produced souvenirs?	จะซื้อที่ระลึกที่ทำใน ท้องถิ่นได้ที่ไหน jà séu têe rá-léuk têe tam nai tórng tìn dâi têe năi

In the Shop

I'd like to buy (an adaptor plug).	อยากจะซื้อ (ปลั๊กต่อ) yàhk jà séu (ʉlák dòr)
I'm just looking.	ดูเฉยๆ doo chĕu·i chĕu·i
Can I look at it?	ขอดูได้ไหม kŏr doo dâi măi
Do you have any others?	มีอีกไหม mee èek măi

PHRASE BUILDER
....
I'd like ..., please.	อยากจะ ... ครับ/ค่ะ	yàhk jà ... kráp/ kâ m/f
a refund	ได้เงินคืน	dâi ngeun keun
to return this	เอามาคืน	ow mah keun

It's faulty.	มันบกพร่อง
	man bòk prôrng
Could I have it wrapped?	ห่อให้ได้ไหม
	hòr hâi dâi măi
Could I have a bag, please?	ขอถุงด้วย
	kŏr tŭng dôo·ay

Paying & Bargaining

How much is it?	เท่าไรครับ/คะ
	tôw-rai kráp/ká m/f
It costs XXX.	ราคา...บาท
	rah-kah...bàht

PHRASE BUILDER

Do you accept ...?	รับ ... ไหม	ráp ... măi
credit cards	บัตรเครดิต	bàt krair-dìt
debit cards	บัตรธนาคาร	bàt tá-nah-kahn

Can you write down the price?	เขียนราคาให้หน่อยได้ไหม
	kĕe·an rah-kah hâi nòy dâi măi
That's too expensive.	แพงไป
	paang bai
Do you have something cheaper?	มีถูกกว่านี้ไหม
	mee tòok gwàh née măi
Can you lower the price?	ลดราคาได้ไหม
	lót rah-kah dâi măi
I'll give you (500 baht).	จะให้ (ห้าร้อยบาท)
	jà hâi (hâh róy bàht)

| I'd like my change, please. | อยากจะได้เงินทอน ครับ/ค่ะ
yàhk jà dâi ngeun torn kráp/
kâ m/f |
| Could I have a receipt, please? | ขอใบเสร็จด้วย
kŏr bai sèt dôo·ay |

Clothes & Shoes

I'm looking for shoes/ underwear.	กำลังหาร้องเท้า/เสื้อชั้นใน gam-lang hăh rorng tów/sêu·a chán nai
Can I try it on?	ลองได้ไหม lorng dâi măi
It doesn't fit.	ไม่ถูกขนาด mâi tòok kà-nàht

PHRASE BUILDER

My size is ...	ฉันใช้ขนาด ...	chăn chái kà-nàht ...
small	เล็ก	lék
medium	กลาง	glahng
large	ใหญ่	yài

Books & Reading

| Do you have a book by (Sulak Sivarak)? | มีหนังสือโดย (อาจารย์ สุลักษณ์
ศิวรักษ์) ไหม
mee năng-sĕu doy (ah-jahn sù-lák
sì-wá-rák) măi |

Is there an English-language bookshop?	มีร้านขายหนังสือภาษาอังกฤษไหม mee ráhn kǎi nǎng-sěu pah-sǎh ang-grìt mǎi
Is there an English-language section?	มีแผนกภาษาอังกฤษไหม mee pà-nàak pah-sǎh ang-grìt mǎi
I'd like a newspaper (in English).	ต้องการหนังสือพิมพ์ (ภาษาอังกฤษ) đôrng gahn nǎng-sěu pim (pah-sǎh ang-grìt)

Music & DVDs

I'm looking for something by (Carabao).	กำลังหาชุดเพลง (วงคาราบาว) gam-lang hǎh chút pleng (wong kah-rah-bow)
What's their best recording?	เพลงชุดไหนเป็นชุดที่ดีที่สุดของเขา pleng chút nǎi ɓen chút têe dee têe sùt kǒrng kǒw
Can I listen to this?	ฟังได้ไหม fang dâi mǎi
What region is this DVD for?	แผ่นดีวีดีนี้สำหรับเขตไหน pàan dee wee dee née sǎm-ràp kèt nǎi

PHRASE BUILDER

I'd like a ...	ต้องการ ...	đôrng gahn ...
CD	แผ่นซีดี	pàan see-dee
DVD	แผ่นดีวีดี	pàan dee-wee-dee

63

Entertainment

Fast Phrases

What's on tonight?	มีอะไรทำ คืนนี้ mee à-rai tam keun née
Where can I find clubs?	จะหา ไนท์คลับ ได้ที่ไหน jà hǎh nai kláp dâi têe nǎi
Where/when shall we meet?	จะพบกันที่ไหน/เมื่อไร jà póp gan têe nǎi/mêu·a rai

Going Out

Where shall we go?	จะไปไหนกันดี ja bai nǎi gan dee

PHRASE BUILDER

Where can I find ...?	จะหา ... ได้ที่ไหน	jà hǎh ... dâi têe nǎi
clubs	ไนท์คลับ	nai kláp
gay venues	สถานบันเทิง สำหรับคนเกย์	sà-tǎhn ban-teung sǎm-ràp kon gair
places to eat	ที่ทานอาหาร	têe tahn ah-hǎhn
pubs	ผับ	pàp

What's on locally?	มีอะไรทำ แถวๆ นี้ mee à-rai tam tăe·ou tăe·ou née
Is there a local entertainment guide?	มีคู่มือ สถานบันเทิงสำหรับแถวนี้ไหม mee kôo meu sà-tăhn ban- teung săm-ràp tăe·ou née măi
What's there to do in the evenings?	มีอะไรบ้างให้ทำตอนเย็น mee à-rai bâhng hâi tam đorn yen
Do you know a good restaurant?	รู้จักร้านอาหารดีๆไหม róo jàk ráhn ah-hăhn dee dee măi

PHRASE BUILDER

I feel like going to a ...	ผม/ดิฉัน รู้สึก อยากจะไป ...	pŏm/dì-chăn róo-sèuk yàhk jà bai ... m/f
bar	บาร์	bah
café	ร้านกาแฟ	ráhn gah-faa
concert	ดูการแสดง	doo gahn sà-daang
film	ดูหนัง	doo năng
full moon party	งานปาร์ตี้พระจันทร์ เต็มดวง	ngahn bah-đee prá jan đem doo·ang
karaoke bar	คาราโอเกะ	kah-rah-oh-gé
nightclub	ไนท์คลับ	nai kláp
party	งานปาร์ตี้	ngahn bah-đee
performance	ดูงานแสดง	doo ngahn sà- daang
pub	ผับ	pàp
restaurant	ร้านอาหาร	ráhn ah-hăhn

Local Knowledge

Put a Smile on Your Dial

Thailand has been called the Land of Smiles, and not without reason. It's cool to smile, and Thai people seem to smile and laugh at the oddest times (such as if you trip over something or make a mistake). It's important to realise that they're not laughing at you, but with you: it's a way of releasing the tension of embarrassment and saying it's OK.

Thais feel negative emotions just as much as anyone else, but the culture does not encourage the outward expression of them. It's considered bad form to blow up in anger in public, and trying to intimidate someone into doing what you want with a loud voice and red face will only make you look bad.

What's on this weekend?	มีอะไรทำเสาร์อาทิตย์นี้ mee à-rai tam sǒw ah-tít née
What's on today?	มีอะไรทำวันนี้ mee à-rai tam wan née
What's on tonight?	มีอะไรทำคืนนี้ mee à-rai tam keun née

Meeting Up

What time will we meet?	จะพบกันกี่โมง jà póp gan gèe mohng
Where will we meet?	จะพบกันที่ไหน jà póp gan têe nǎi
Let's meet at (eight pm).	พบกัน (สองทุ่ม) ดีไหม póp gan (sǒrng tûm) dee mǎi
Let's meet at the (entrance).	พบกัน ที่ (ทางเข้า) ดีไหม póp gan têe (tahng kôw) dee mǎi

Practicalities

≡ Fast Phrases

Where's the nearest ATM?	ตู้เอทีเอ็มที่ใกล้ที่สุดอยู่ที่ไหน dôo air-tee-em têe glâi têe sùt yòo têe năi
Is there wireless internet access here?	ที่นี่มีไวไฟไหม têe née mee wai fai măi
Where's the toilet?	ห้องส้วมอยู่ไหน hôrng sôo·am yòo năi

Banking

Where's a bank?	ธนาคารอยู่ที่ไหน tá-nah-kahn yòo têe năi
What time does the bank open?	ธนาคารเปิดกี่โมง tá-nah-kahn bèut gèe mohng
Where can I change money?	แลกเงินได้ที่ไหน lâak ngeun dâi têe năi

PHRASE BUILDER

Where's ...?	... อยู่ที่ไหน	... yòo têe năi
an ATM	ตู้เอทีเอ็ม	dôo air-tee-em
a foreign exchange office	ที่แลกเงินต่าง ประเทศ	têe lâak ngeun dàhng brà-têt

67

Fast Talk

Understanding Thai

Most sentences are composed of several words (or parts of words) serving various grammatical functions, as well as those that carry meaning (primarily nouns and verbs). If you're finding it hard to understand what someone is saying to you, listen out for the nouns and verbs to work out the context – this shouldn't be hard as they are usually more emphasised in speech. If you're still having trouble, a useful phrase to know is pôot cháa cháa dâi măi พูดช้าๆได้ไหม (Please speak more slowly).

Where can I withdraw money?	ถอนเงิน ได้ที่ไหน tŏrn ngeun dâi têe năi
I'd like to withdraw money.	อยากจะ ถอนเงิน yàhk jà tŏrn ngeun
What's the charge for that?	ค่าธรรมเนียม เท่าไร kâh tam-nee·am tôw-rai
What's the exchange rate?	อัตราแลกเปลี่ยน เท่าไร àt-đrah lâak ป lèe·an tôw-rai

Phone/Mobile Phone

Where's the nearest public phone?	ตู้โทรศัพท์ที่ใกล้เคียง อยู่ที่ไหน đôo toh-rá-sàp têe glâi kee·ang yòo têe năi
I want to buy a phonecard.	อยากจะ ซื้อบัตรโทรศัพท์ yàhk jà séu bàt toh-rá-sàp
I want to call (Singapore).	อยากจะ โทรไปประเทศ (สิงคโปร์) yàhk jà toh ไ bai ป rà-têt (sĭng-ká-ป boh)

I want to reverse the charges.	อยากจะ โทรเก็บปลายทาง yàhk jà toh gèp ไblai tahng
How much does a (three)-minute call cost?	โทร (สาม) นาทีคิดเงินเท่าไร toh (săhm) nah-tee kít ngeun tôw-rai
The number is ...	เบอร์ก็คือ ... beu gôr keu ...
I've been cut off.	สายหลุดแล้ว săi lùt láa·ou
I'd like a charger for my phone.	ต้อง การ เครื่องชาร์จโทรศัพท์ đôrng gahn krêu·ang cháht toh-rá-sàp
I'd like a SIM card.	ต้อง การ บัตรซิม đôrng gahn bàt sim
I'd like to buy (an adaptor plug).	อยากจะซื้อ (ปลั๊กต่อ) yàhk jà séu (ไblák đòr)

Internet

Where's the local Internet café?	ที่ไหนร้านอินเตอร์เนตที่ใกล้เคีย têe năi ráhn in-đeu-nét têe glâi kee·ang

PHRASE BUILDER

How much per ...?	คิด ... ละเท่าไร	kít ... lá tôw-rai
hour	ชั่วโมง	chôo·a mohng
(five)-minutes	(ห้า) นาที	(hâh) nah-tee
page	หน้า	nâh

Is there wireless internet access here?	ที่นี่มีไวไฟไหม têe née mee wai fai măi
Can I connect my laptop here?	ต่อแล็บทอบที่นี่ได้ไหม đor láap tóp têe née dâi măi
Do you have headphones (with a microphone)?	มีหูฟัง(ที่มีไมค์) ไหม mee hŏo fang (têe mee mai) măi
Can I connect my camera to this computer?	ต่อกล้องกับคอมพิวเตอร์นี้ได้ไหม đòr glôrng gàp korm-pew-đeu née dâi măi
It's crashed.	เครื่องแฮ้งแล้ว krêu·ang háang láa·ou
I've finished.	เสร็จแล้ว sèt láa·ou

PHRASE BUILDER

I'd like to ...	อยากจะ ...	yàhk jà ...
check my email	ตรวจอีเมล	đròo·at ee-mairn
use a printer	ใช้เครื่อพิมพ์	chái krêu·ang pim
use a scanner	ใช้เครื่อสแกน	chái krêu·ang sà·gaan

Emergencies

Help!	ช่วยด้วย chôo·ay dôo·ay
Stop!	หยุด yùt

Go away!	ไปให้พ้น ฺฺbai hâi pón
Leave me alone!	อย่ายุ่งกับฉัน yàh yûng gàp chăn
Thief!	ขโมย kà-moy
Fire!	ไฟไหม้ fai mâi
Watch out!	ระวัง rá-wang
It's an emergency.	เป็นเหตุฉุกเฉิน ฺben hèt chùk-chĕun
Call a doctor!	ตามหมอหน่อย ฺdahm mŏr nòy
Call an ambulance!	ตามรถพยาบาล ฺdahm rót pá-yah-bahn
Call the police!	เรียกตำรวจมา rêe·ak ฺdam-ròo·at mah
Could you please help?	ช่วยได้ไหม chôo·ay dâi măi
Can I use your phone?	ใช้โทรศัพท์ของคุณได้ไหม chái toh-rá-sàp kŏrng kun dâi măi
I'm lost.	ผม/ดิฉัน หลงทาง pŏm/dì-chăn lŏng tahng m/f
Where are the toilets?	ห้องน้ำอยู่ที่ไหน hôrng nám yòo têe năi

Police

Where's the police station?	สถานีตำรวจอยู่ที่ไหน sà-tăh-nee đam-ròo·at yòo têe năi
I've been raped.	ผม/ดิฉันโดนข่มขืน pŏm/dì-chăn dohn kòm kĕun m/f
I've been robbed.	ผม/ดิฉันโดนขโมย pŏm/dì-chăn dohn kà-moy m/f
My ... was stolen.	...ของ ผม/ดิฉันถูกขโมย ... kŏrng pŏm dì-chăn tòok kà-moy m/f

PHRASE BUILDER

I've lost my ...	ผม/ดิฉัน ทำ ... หายแล้ว	pŏm/dì-chăn tam ... hăi láa·ou m/f
bags	กระเป๋า	grà-ƀŏw
money	เงิน	ngeun
passport	หนังสือเดินทาง	năng-sĕu deun tahng

I want to contact my embassy.	ผม/ดิฉัน อยากจะติดต่อสถานทูต pŏm/dì-chăn yàhk jà đit đòr sà-tăhn tôot m/f
I want to contact my consulate.	ผม/ดิฉัน อยากจะติดต่อกงศุล pŏm/dì-chăn yàhk jà đit đòr gong-sŭn m/f
I have insurance.	ผม/ดิฉันมีประกันอยู่ pŏm/dì-chăn mee ƀrà-gan yòo m/f

Health

Where's the nearest chemist?	ร้านขายยา ที่ใกล้เคียง อยู่ที่ไหน ráhn kăi yah têe glâi kee·ang yòo têe năi
Where's the nearest dentist?	หมอฟันที่ใกล้เคียง อยู่ที่ไหน mŏr fan têe glâi kee·ang yòo têe năi
Where's the nearest hospital?	โรงพยาบาลที่ใกล้เคียง อยู่ที่ไหน rohng pá-yah-bahn têe glâi kee·ang yòo têe năi
I need a doctor (who speaks English).	ผม/ดิฉัน ต้องการหมอ (ที่พูด ภาษาอังกฤษได้) pŏm/dì-chăn dôrng gahn mŏr (têe pôot pah-săh ang-grìt dâi) m/f
Could I see a female doctor?	พบกับคุณหมอผู้หญิงได้ไหม póp gàp kun mŏr pôo yĭng âi măi
My prescription is ...	มีใบสั่งยาสำหรับ... mee bai sàng yah săm-ràp
I need something for ...	ต้องการยาสำหรับ... dôrng gahn yah săm-ràp ...

PHRASE BUILDER

I feel ...	ผม/ดิฉันรู้สึก ...	pŏm/dì-chăn róo-sèuk ... m/f
dizzy	เวียนหัว	wee·an hŏo·a
nauseous	คลื่นไส้	klêun sâi
hot and cold	หนาว ๆ ร้อน ๆ	nŏw nŏw rórn rórn
weak	อ่อนเพลีย	òrn plee·a

Symptoms, Conditions & Allergies

I'm sick.	ผม/ดิฉันป่วย pŏm/dì-chăn bòo·ay m/f
It hurts here.	เจ็บตรงนี้ jèp drong née
I've been injured.	ผม/ดิฉัน บาดเจ็บ pŏm/dì-chăn bàht jèp m/f
I've been vomiting.	ผม/ดิฉัน อาเจียน pŏm/dì-chăn ah-jee·an m/f
I'm allergic to antibiotics.	ผม/ดิฉันแพ้ยาปฏิชีวนะ pŏm/dì-chăn páa yah bà-dì-chee-wá-ná m/f
I'm allergic to aspirin.	ผม/ดิฉันแพ้ยาแอสไพริน pŏm/dì-chăn páa yah àat-sà-pai-rin m/f
I'm allergic to penicillin.	ผม/ดิฉันแพ้ยาเพนนิซิลลิน pŏm/dì-chăn páa yah pen-ní-sin-lin m/f

PHRASE BUILDER

I have (a/an) ...	ผม/ดิฉัน ...	pŏm/dì-chăn ... m/f
cough	เป็นไอ	ben ai
fever	เป็นไข้	ben kâi
heatstroke	แพ้แดด	páa dàat
malaria	เป็นไข้มาเลเรีย	ben kâi mah-lair-ree·a

Dictionary

ENGLISH *to* THAI

The symbols ⓝ, ⓐ and ⓥ (indicating noun, adjective and verb) have been added for clarity where an English term could be either.

a

commodation ที่พัก têe pák
count บัญชี ban-chee
roplane เครื่องบิน krêu·ang bin
ternoon ตอนบ่าย dorn bài
-conditioned ปรับอากาศ ่bràp
-gàht
port สนามบิน sà·năhm bin
port tax ภาษีสนามบิน pah-sĕe
-năhm bin
arm clock นาฬิกาปลุก nah-lí-gah ่blùk
cohol เหล้า lôw
tique วัตถุโบราณ wát-tù boh-rahn
pointment การนัด gahn nát
t gallery ห้องแสดงภาพ hôrng sà-
ang pâhp
htray ที่เขี่ยบุหรี่ têe kèe·a bù-rèe

at

at ที่ têe
automated teller machine (ATM)
ตู้เอทีเอ็ม ่dôo air tee em
autumn หน้าใบไม้ร่วง nâh bai mái
rôo·ang

b

baby ทารก tah-rók
back (body) หลัง lăng
backpack เป้ ่bâir
bad เลว le·ou
bag ถุง tŭng
baggage กระเป๋า grà-่bŏw
baggage allowance พิกัดน้ำหนักกระเป๋า
pí-gàt nám nàk grà-่bŏw
baggage claim ที่รับกระเป๋า têe ráp
grà-่bŏw

75

bakery ที่ขายขนมปัง tée kăi kà-nŏm bang

Band-Aid ปลาสเตอร์ blah-sà-đeu

bank ธนาคาร tá-nah-kahn

bathroom ห้องน้ำ hông nám

battery (flashlight) ถ่านไฟฉาย tàhn fai chăi

battery (car) หม้อแบตเตอรี่ môr bàat-deu-rêe

beach ชายหาด chai hàht

beautiful สวย sŏo-ay

beauty salon ร้านเสริมสวย ráhn sĕum sŏo-ay

bed เตียง đee-ang

bed linen ผ้าปูที่นอน pâh boo tée norn

bedroom ห้องนอน hông norn

beer เบียร์ bee-a

bicycle รถจักรยาน rót jàk-gà-yahn

big ใหญ่ yài

bill (restaurant etc) บิลค์ bin

birthday วันเกิด wan gèut

black สีดำ sĕe dam

blanket ผ้าห่ม pâh hòm

blood group กลุ่มเลือด glum lêu-at

blue (light) สีฟ้า sĕe fáh

blue (dark) สีน้ำเงิน sĕe nám ngeun

boarding house บ้านพัก bâhn pák

boarding pass บัตรขึ้นเครื่องบิน bàt kêun krêu-ang bin

boat เรือ reu-a

book หนังสือ năng-sĕu

book (make a booking) จอง jorng

book shop ร้านขายหนังสือ ráhn kăi năng-sĕu

booked out จองเต็มแล้ว jorng đem láa-ou

border ชายแดน chai daan

bottle ขวด kòo-at

box กล่อง glòrng

boy เด็กชาย dèk chai

boyfriend แฟนผู้ชาย faan pôo chai

bra ยกทรง yók song

brakes เบรก brèk

bread ขนมปัง kà-nŏm bang

briefcase กระเป๋าเอกสาร grà-bŏw èk-gà-săhn

broken หักแล้ว hàk láa-ou

brother (older) พี่ชาย pêe chai

brother (younger) น้องชาย nórng cha

brown สีน้ำตาล sĕe nám đahn

building ตึก đèuk

bus (city) รถเมล์ rót mair

bus (intercity) รถบัส rót bàt

bus station สถานีขนส่ง sà-tăh-nee kŏn sòng

bus stop ป้ายรถเมล์ bâi rót mair

business ธุรกิจ tú-rá-gìt

business class ชั้นธุรกิจ chán tú-rá-gìt

busy ยุ่ง yûng

butcher's shop ร้านขายเนื้อ ráhn kăi néu-a

c

café ร้านกาแฟ ráhn gah-faa

call เรียก rêe-ak

camera กล้องถ่ายรูป glôrng tài rôop

can (be able) เป็น ben

can (have permission) ได้ dâi

can (tin) กระป๋อง grà-bŏrng

cancel ยกเลิก yók lêuk

car รถยนต์ rót yon

car hire การเช่ารถ gahn chôw rót

car owner's title ใบกรรมสิทธิ์รถยนต์ bai gam-má-sìt rót yon

car park ที่จอดรถ tée jòrt rót

car registration ทะเบียนรถ tá-bee-an rót

cash เงินสด ngeun sòt

cashier แคเชียร์ kaa-chee-a

change ⓥ การเปลี่ยนแปลง gahn blèe-an blaang

change (coins) เงินปลีก ngeun blèek

change (money) แลก lâak

check (banking) เช็ค chék

check-in (desk) เช็คอิน chék in

cheque (banking) เช็ค chék

child เด็ก dèk

church โบสถ์ bòht
cigarette lighter ไฟแช็ค fai cháak
city เมือง meu·ang
city centre ใจกลางเมือง jai glahng meu·ang
clean ⓐ สะอาด sà·àht
cleaning การทำสะอาด gahn tam sà·àht
cloakroom ห้องเก็บเสื้อ hôrng gèp sêu·a
closed ปิดแล้ว bìt láa·ou
clothing เสื้อผ้า sêu·a pâh
coat เสื้อคลุม sêu·a klum
coffee กาแฟ gah·faa
coins เหรียญ rěe·an
cold เย็น yen
comfortable สบาย sà·bai
company บริษัท bor·rí·sàt
computer คอมพิวเตอร์ korm·pew·đeu
condom ถุงยางอนามัย tǔng yahng à·nah·mai
confirm (a booking) ยืนยัน yeun yan
connection ข้อต่อ kôr đòr
convenience store ร้านขายของชำ ráhn kǎi kǒrng cham
cook ⓝ คนครัว kon kroo·a
cook ⓥ ทำอาหาร tam ah·hǎhn
cool เย็น yen
cough ไอ ai
countryside ชนบท chon·ná·bot
cover charge ค่าผ่านประตู kâh pàhn bprà·đoo
crafts หัตถกรรม hàt·tà·gam
credit card บัตรเครดิต bàt crair·dìt
currency exchange การแลกเงิน gahn lâak ngeun
customs ศุลกากร sǔn·lá·gah·gorn

d

daily รายวัน rai wan
date (day) วันที่ wan têe
date of birth วันที่เกิด wan têe gèut
daughter ลูกสาว lôok sǒw

day วัน wan
day after tomorrow (the) วันมะรืน wan má·reun
day before yesterday (the) เมื่อวานซืน mêu·a wahn seun
delay การเสียเวลา gahn sěe·a wair·lah
depart (leave) ออกเดินทาง òrk deun tahng
department store สรรพสินค้า sàp·pá·sǐn·káh
departure ขาออก kǎh òrk
diaper ผ้าอ้อม pâh ôrm
dictionary พจนานุกรม pót·jà·nah·nú·grom
dining car ตู้รับประทานอาหาร đoo ráp bprà·tahn ah·hǎhn
dinner อาหารมื้อเย็น ah·hǎhn méu yen
direct ทางตรง tahng đrong
dirty สกปรก sòk·gà·bròk
discount ราคาส่วนลด rah·kah sòo·an lót
dish จาน jahn
doctor หมอ mǒr
dog หมา mǎh
double bed เตียงคู่ đee·ang kôo
double room ห้องคู่ hôrng kôo
dress กระโปรง grà·bprohng
drink ⓝ เครื่องดื่ม krêu·ang dèum
drink ⓥ ดื่ม dèum
drivers licence ใบขับขี่ bai kàp kèe
drunk เมา mow
dry ⓐ แห้ง hâang

e

each แต่ละ đàa·lá
early เช้า chów
east ทิศตะวันออก tít đà·wan òrk
eat (informal) กิน gin
eat (polite) ทาน tahn
eat (very formal) รับประทาน ráp bprà·tahn
economy class ชั้นประหยัด chán bprà·yàt

elevator ลิฟต์ lip
embassy สถานทูต sà-tǎhn tôot
English อังกฤษ ang-grìt
enough พอ por
entry การเข้า gahn kôw
envelope ซองจดหมาย sorng jòt-mǎi
evening ตอนเย็น dorn yen
every ทุก túk
everything ทุกสิ่ง túk sìng
excess (baggage) (น้ำหนัก)เกิน (nám nàk) geun
exchange ⓝ การแลกเปลี่ยน gahn lâak bìee-an
exchange ⓥ แลกเปลี่ยน lâak bìee-an
exhibition นิทรรศการ ní-tát-sà-gahn
exit ⓝ ทางออก tahng òrk
expensive แพง paang
express mail (by) ไปรษณีย์ด่วน bprai-sà-nee dòo-an

f

fall (autumn) หน้าใบไม้ร่วง nâh bai mái rôo-ang
family ครอบครัว krôrp kroo-a
fare ค่าโดยสาร kâh doy sǎhn
fashion แฟชั่น faa-chân
fast เร็ว re-ou
father inf พ่อ pôr
father pol บิดา bì-dah
ferry เรือข้ามฟาก reu-a kâhm fâhk
fever ไข้ kâi
film (cinema) ภาพยนตร์ pâhp-pá-yon
film (for camera) ฟิล์ม fim
fine (penalty) ค่าปรับ kâh bràp
finger นิ้ว néw
first class ชั้นหนึ่ง chán nèung
fish shop ร้านขายปลา ráhn kǎi plah
fleamarket ตลาดขายของเบ็ดเตล็ด dà-làht kǎi kǒrng bèt dà-lèt
flight เที่ยวบิน têe-o bin
floor (storey) ชั้น chán
flu ไข้หวัด kâi wàt
footpath ทางเดิน tahng deun

foreign ต่างชาติ dàhng châht
forest ป่า bàh
free (not bound) อิสระ ìt-sà-rà
free (of charge) ฟรี free
fresh สด sòt
friend เพื่อน pêu-an

g

garden สวน sǒo-an
gas (for cooking) ก๊าซ gáht
gas (petrol) น้ำมันเบนซิน nám-man ben-sin
gift ของขวัญ kǒrng kwǎn
girl สาว sǒw
girlfriend แฟนสาว faan sǒw
glasses แว่นตา wâan dah
glove(s) ถุงมือ tǔng meu
go ไป bai
go out ไปข้างนอก bai kâhng nôrk
go shopping ไปซื้อของ bai séu kǒrng
gold ทองคำ torng kam
grateful ปลื้มใจ blêum jai
gray สีเทา sěe tow
green สีเขียว sěe kěe-o
grocery ร้านขายของชำ ráhn kǎi kǒrng cham
guesthouse บ้านพัก bâhn pák
guided tour ทัวร์ too-a

h

half ครึ่ง krêung
handsome รูปหล่อ rôop lòr
heated เร่าร้อน rôw rórn
help ⓝ ความช่วยเหลือ kwahm chôo-ay lěu-a
help ⓥ ช่วย chôo-ay
here ที่นี่ têe nêe
highway ทางหลวง tahng lǒo-ang
hire เช่า chôw
holiday (public) วันหยุด wan yùt
holidays การพักร้อน gahn pák rórn

honeymoon ดื่มน้ำผึ้งพระจันทร์ dèum nám pêung prá jan
hot ร้อน rórn
hot (spicy) เผ็ด pèt
hot springs บ่อน้ำร้อน bòr nám rórn
hot water น้ำร้อน nám rórn
hotel โรงแรม rohng raam
hour ชั่วโมง chôo·a mohng
husband ผัว pŏo·a

i

identification หลักฐาน làk tăhn
identification card (ID) บัตรประจำตัว bàt brà-jam đoo·a
ill ป่วย bòo·ay
included รวมด้วย roo·am dôo·ay
information ข้อมูล kôr moon
insurance การประกัน gahn brà-gan
interpreter ล่าม lâhm
itinerary รายการเดินทาง rai gahn deun tahng

j

jacket เสื้อกันหนาว sêu·a gan nŏw
jeans กางเกงยีน gahng geng yeen
jewellery เครื่องเพชรพลอย krêu·ang pét ploy
journey การเดินทาง gahn deun tahng
jumper (sweater) เสื้อถัก sêu·a tàk

k

key ลูกกุญแจ lôok gun-jaa
kind ใจดี jai dee
kitchen ครัว kroo·a

l

lane ซอย soy
large ใหญ่ yài
last (previous) ที่แล้ว tee láaw

late ช้า cháh
later ทีหลัง tee lăng
launderette โรงซักรีด rohng sák rêet
laundry (clothes) ผ้าซัก pâh sák
leather หนัง năng
left luggage (office) ห้องรับฝากกระเป๋า hôrng ráp fàhk grá-bŏw
letter (mail) จดหมาย jòt-măi
lift (elevator) ลิฟต์ líp
linen (material) ผ้าลินิน pâh lí-nin
locked ใส่กุญแจแล้ว sài gun-jaa láa·ou
look for หา hăh
lost หาย hăi
lost property office ที่แจ้งของหาย tee jâang kŏrng hăi
luggage กระเป๋า grà-bŏw
luggage lockers ตู้ฝากกระเป๋า đôo fàhk grà-bŏw
lunch อาหารกลางวัน ah-hăhn glahng wan

m

mail (postal system) ไปรษณีย์ brai-sà-nee
make-up เครื่องสำอาง krêu·ang săm-ahng
man ผู้ชาย pôo chai
manager ผู้จัดการ pôo jàt gahn
map แผนที่ păan têe
market ตลาด đà-làht
meal มื้ออาหาร méu ah-hăhn
meat เนื้อ néu·a
medicine (medication) ยา yah
metro station สถานีรถไฟใต้ดิน sà-tăh-nee rót fai dâi din
midday เที่ยงวัน têe·ang wan
midnight เที่ยงคืน têe·ang keun
milk น้ำนม nám nom
mineral water น้ำแร่ nám râa
mobile phone โทรศัพท์มือถือ toh-rá-sàp meu těu
modem โมเดม moh-dem
money เงิน ngeun

month เดือน deu·an
morning ตอนเช้า dorn chów
mother inf แม่ mâae
mother pol มารดา mahn-dah
motorcycle รถมอเตอร์ไซค์ rót mor-deu-sai
motorway (tollway) ทางด่วน tahng dòo·an
mountain ภูเขา poo kŏw
museum พิพิธภัณฑ์ pí-pít-tá-pan
music shop ร้านดนตรี ráhn don-dree

n

name ชื่อ chêu
napkin ผ้าเช็ดปาก pâh chét bàhk
nappy ผ้าอ้อม pâh ôrm
newsagency ร้านขายหนังสือพิมพ์ ráhn kăi năng-sĕu pim
next (month) หน้า nâh
nice (food only) อร่อย à-ròy
night คืน keun
night out เที่ยวกลางคืน têe·o glahng keun
nightclub ไนท์คลับ nai kláp
no vacancy ไม่มีห้องว่าง mâi mee hôrng wâhng
non-smoking ไม่สูบบุหรี่ mâi sòop bù-rèe
noon เที่ยง têe·ang
north ทิศเหนือ tit nĕu·a
now เดี๋ยวนี้ dĕe·o née
number (figure) หมายเลข măi lêk
number (quantity) จำนวน jam-noo·an
nurse (female) นางพยาบาล nahng pá-yah-bahn
nurse (male) บุรุษพยาบาล bù-rút pá-yah-bahn

o

oil น้ำมัน nám man

one-way (ticket) เที่ยวเดียว têe·o dee·o
open ⓐ&ⓥ เปิด bèut
opening hours เวลาเปิด wair-lah bèut
orange (colour) สีส้ม sĕe sôm
out of order เสีย sĕe·a

p

painter ช่างทาสี châhng tah sĕe
painting (a work) ภาพเขียน pâhp kĕe·an
painting (the art) จิตรกรรม jìt-drà-gam
pants (trousers) กางเกง gahng-geng
pantyhose ถุงน่อง tŭng nôrng
paper กระดาษ grà-dàht
party (night out) งานเลี้ยง ngahn lée·ang
passenger ผู้โดยสาร pôo doy săhn
passport หนังสือเดินทาง năng-sĕu deun tahng
passport number หมายเลขหนังสือเดินทาง măi lêk năng-sĕu deun tahng
path ทาง tahng
pensioner คนกินเงินบำนาญ kon gin ngeun bam-nahn
performance งานแสดง ngahn sà-daang
petrol เบนซิน ben-sin
petrol station ปั๊มน้ำมัน bám nám-man
phone book สมุดโทรศัพท์ sà-mùt toh-rá-sàp
phone box ตู้โทรศัพท์ đôo toh-rá-sàp
phone card บัตรโทรศัพท์ bàt toh-rá-sàp
phrasebook คู่มือสนทนา kôo meu sŏn-tá-nah
picnic ปิกนิก bìk-nik
pillow หมอน mŏrn
pillowcase ปลอกหมอน blòrk mŏrn
pink สีชมพู sĕe chom-poo
platform ชานชาลา chahn chah-lah

police officer นายตำรวจ nai dam-ròo·at

police station สถานีตำรวจ sà-tăh-nee dam-ròo·at

post code รหัสไปรษณีย์ rá-hàt brai-sà-nee

pound (money, weight) ปอนด์ born

prescription ใบสั่งยา bai sàng yah

present (gift) ของขวัญ kŏrng kwăn

price ราคา rah-kah

q

quick เร็ว re·ou

r

receipt ใบเสร็จ bai sèt

red สีแดง sĕe daang

refund เงินคืน ngeun keun

rent เช่า chôw

repair ซ่อม sôrm

retired ปลดเกษียณ blòt gà-sĕe·an

return (ticket) ไปกลับ bai glàp

return (come back) กลับ glàp

road ถนน tà-nŏn

rob ขโมย kà-moy

room ห้อง hôrng

room number หมายเลขห้อง măi lêk hôrng

route สาย săi

s

safe ⓝ ตู้เซฟ dôo sép

safe ⓐ ปลอดภัย blòrt pai

sea ทะเล tá-lair

season หน้า nâh

seat (place) ที่นั่ง têe nâng

seatbelt เข็มขัดนิรภัย kĕm kàt ní-rá-pai

service การบริการ gahn bor-ri-gahn

service charge ค่าบริการ kâh bor-ri-gahn

share (a dorm etc) รวมกันใช้ rôo·am gan chái

share (with) แบ่ง bàang

shirt เสื้อเชิ้ต sêu·a chéut

shoe รองเท้า rorng tów

shop ⓝ ร้าน ráhn

shop ⓥ ซื้อของ séu kŏrng

shopping centre สรรพสินค้า sàp-pá-sĭn-káh

short (height) เตี้ย dêe·a

show ⓝ งานแสดง ngahn sà-daang

show ⓥ แสดง sà-daang

shower ฝักบัว fàk boo·a

sick ป่วย bòo·ay

silver เงิน ngeun

single (person) โสด sòht

single room ห้องเดี่ยว hôrng dèe·o

sister (older) พี่สาว pêe sŏw

sister (younger) น้องสาว nórng sŏw

size (general) ขนาด kà-nàht

skirt กระโปรง grà-brohng

Skytrain station สถานีรถไฟฟ้า sà-tăh-nee rót fai fáh

sleeping bag ถุงนอน tŭng norn

slide (film) ฟิล์มสไลด์ fim sà-lái

smoke ⓥ ควัน kwan

snack ⓝ อาหารว่าง ah-hăhn wâhng

snow ⓝ หิมะ hì-má

sock(s) ถุงเท้า tŭng tów

son ลูกชาย lôok chai

soon เร็ว ๆ นี้ re·ou re·ou née

south ทิศใต้ tít dâi

spring (season) หน้าใบไม้ผลิ nâh bai mái plì

stairway บันได ban-dai

stamp แสตมป์ sà-đáam

stationer's (shop) ร้านขายอุปกรณ์เขียน ráhn kăi ùp-bà-gorn kĕe·an

stolen ขโมยแล้ว kà-moy láa·ou

street ถนน tà-nŏn

student นักศึกษา nák sèuk-săh

subtitles คำบรรยาย kam ban-yai

suitcase กระเป๋าเดินทาง grà-bŏw deun tahng

summer หน้าร้อน nâh rórn
supermarket ซูเปอร์มาร์เก็ต soo·beu·mah·gèt
surface mail ไปรษณีย์ทางธรรมดา brai·sà·nee tahng tam·má·dah
surname นามสกุล nahm sà·gun
sweater เสื้อถัก sêu·a tàk
swim ⓥ ว่ายน้ำ wâi nám
swimming pool สระว่ายน้ำ sà wâi nám

t

tall สูง sŏong
taxi stand ที่จอดรถแท็กซี่ têe jòrt rót táak·sêe
ticket ตั๋ว dŏo·a
ticket machine เครื่องขายตั๋ว krêu·ang kăi dŏo·a
ticket office ช่องขายตั๋ว chôrng kăi dŏo·a
time เวลา wair·lah
timetable ตารางเวลา đah·rahng wair·lah
tip (gratuity) เงินทิป ngeun típ
to ถึง tĕung
today วันนี้ wan née
together ด้วยกัน dôo·ay gan
tomorrow พรุ่งนี้ prûng née
tour ⓝ ทัวร์ too·a
tourist office สำนักงานท่องเที่ยว săm·nák ngahn tôrng têe·o
towel ผ้าเช็ดตัว pâh chét đoo·a
train รถไฟ rót fai
train station สถานีรถไฟ sà·tăh·nee rót fai
travel agency บริษัทท่องเที่ยว bor·rí·sàt tôrng têe·o
trip (journey) เที่ยว têe·o
trousers กางเกง gahng·geng
twin beds สองเตียง sŏrng đee·ang

u

underwear กางเกงใน gahng·geng nai

v

vacancy ห้องว่าง hôrng wâhng
vacant ว่าง wâhng
vacation เที่ยวพักผ่อน têe·o pák pòrn
validate ทำให้ถูกต้อง tam hâi tòok dôrng
vegetable ผัก pàk
view ⓝ ทิวทัศน์ tew tát

w

walk เดิน deun
warm อุ่น ùn
wash (general) ล้าง láhng
wash (clothes) ซัก sák
wash (hair) สระ sà
washing machine เครื่องซักผ้า krêu·ang sák pâh
watch ⓝ นาฬิกา nah·lí·gah
watch ⓥ ดู doo
water น้ำ nám
way ทาง tahng
west ทิศตะวันตก tít đà·wan đòk
what อะไร à·rai
when เมื่อไร mêu·a rai
where ที่ไหน têe năi
which อันไหน an năi
who ใคร krai
why ทำไม tam mai
wide กว้าง gwâhng
wife เมีย mee·a
window หน้าต่าง nâh đàhng
wine เหล้าไวน์ lôw wai
winter หน้าหนาว nâh nŏw
woman ผู้หญิง pôo yĭng
wrong ผิด pit

y

year ปี bee
yesterday เมื่อวาน mêu·a wahn
youth hostel บ้านเยาวชน bâhn yow·wá·chon

Dictionary

THAI *to* ENGLISH

If you're having trouble understanding Thai, point to the text below. This gives directions on how to look up words in Thai and show you the English translation.

ใช้พจนานุกรมไทย–อังกฤษนี้เพื่อช่วยชาวต่างชาติคนนี้เข้าใจสิ่งที่คุณอยากจะพูดค้นหา ศัพท์จากรายการศัพท์ภาษาไทยแล้วจึงให้เห็นศัพท์ภาษาอังกฤษที่ตรงกับคำศัพท์นั้น

ก

กระดาษ grà-dàht **paper**
กระป๋อง grà-b̌ŏrng **can • tin**
กระเป๋า grà-b̌ŏw **baggage • luggage**
กระเป๋าเดินทาง grà-b̌ŏw deun tahng **suitcase**
กระโปรง grà-b̌rohng **dress • skirt**
กล้องถ่ายรูป glôrng tài rôop **camera**
กลับ glàp **return (come back)**
กลุ่มเลือด glum lêu-at **blood group**
ก๊อกน้ำ górk nám **tap**
กับแกล้ม gàp glâam **drinking food**
กางเกง gahng-geng **pants • trousers**
กางเกงขาสั้น gahng-geng kǎh sân **shorts**
กางเกงใน gahng geng nai **underwear**
กางเกงยีน gahng geng yeen **jeans**
ก๊าซ gáht **gas (for cooking)**

กาแฟ gah-faa **coffee**
การจอง gahn jorng **reservation (booking)**
การช้าเวลา gahn cháh wair-lah **delay**
การเช่ารถ gahn chôw rót **car hire**
การต่อ gahn dòr **connection (transport)**
การถ่ายภาพ gahn tài pâhp **photography**
การทำสะอาด gahn tam sà-àht **cleaning**
การนัด gahn nát **appointment**
การบริการ gahn bor-rí-gahn **service**
การประกัน gahn b̌rà-gan **insurance**
การประชุม gahn b̌rà-chum **conference**
การปรับร่างกายยกับเวลาที่แตกต่าง gahn b̌ràp râhng gai gàp wair-lah têe đàak đàhng **jet lag**
การพักร้อน gahn pák rórn **holidays**
การแลกเงิน gahn lâak ngeun **currency exchange**

การสัมภาษณ์ gahn săm-pâht **interview**
กำรต่อยมวย gahn dòy moo·ay **boxing**
กำหนดความเร็ว gam-nòt kwahm re·ou **speed limit**
ใกล้ glâi **close • near**
ใกล้เคียง glâi kee·ang **nearby**
ใกล้ที่สุด glâi têe-sùt **nearest**
ไกด์ gai **guide (person)**

ข

ขนแกะ kŏn gàa **wool**
ขนมปัง kà-nŏm bang **bread**
ขนาด kà-nàht **size (general)**
ขโมย kà-moy **thief**
ขโมย kà-moy **steal**
ขโมยแล้ว kà-moy láa·ou **stolen**
ขวด kòo·at **bottle**
ขวา kwăh **right (direction)**
ข้อความฝาก kôr kwahm fàhk **message**
ของขวัญ kŏrng kwăn **present (gift)**
ของที่ระลึก kŏrng têe rá-léuk **souvenir**
ข้อต่อ kôr dòr **connection**
ข้อมูล kôr moon **information**
ขอแสดงความยินดี kŏr sà-daang kwahm yin dee **congratulations**
ขาเข้า kăh kôw **arrivals**
ข้างนอก kâhng nôrk **outside**
ข้างใน kâhng nai **inside**
ข้างหลัง kâhng lăng **behind**
ข้างๆ kâhng kâhng **beside**
ข่าว kòw **news**
เข็มขัดนิรภัย kĕm kàt ní-rá-pai **seatbelt**
ไข้ kâi **fever**

ค

คนกินเงินบำนาญ kon gin ngeun bam-nahn **pensioner**
คนกินเจ kon gin jair **vegetarian**
คนครัว kon kroo·a **cook**
ครอบครัว krôrp kroo·a **family**
ควัน kwan **smoke**
คอมพิวเตอร์ korm-pew-đeu **computer**
คอมพิวเตอร์แล็ปท็อป korm-pew-đeu láap-

tórp **laptop**
ค่าบริการ kâh bor-rí-gahn **service charge**
ค่าปรับ kâh bràp **fine (penalty)**
ค่าผ่านประตู kâh pàhn bra-đoo **cover charge**
คำบรรยาย kam ban-yai **subtitles**
คำร้องทุกข์ kam rórng túk **complaint**
คืน keun **night**
คู่มือนำเที่ยว kôo meu nam têe·o **guidebook**
คู่มือสนทนา kôo meu sŏn-tá-nah **phrasebook**
เครื่องซักผ้า krêu·ang sák pâh **washing machine**
เครื่องดื่ม krêu·ang dèum **drink**
เครื่องบริการตั๋ว krêu·ang bor-rí-gahn đŏo·a **ticket machine**
เครื่องบิน krêu·ang bin **aeroplane**
เครื่องเพชรพลอย krêu·ang pét ploy **jewellery**
แคชเชียร์ kaa-chee·a **cashier**
ใคร krai **who**

ง

งานเต้นรำ ngahn đên ram **rave • dance party**
งานเลี้ยง ngahn lée·ang **party**
งานแสดง ngahn sà-daang **show**
เงิน ngeun **money •silver**
เงินคืน ngeun keun **refund**
เงินทิป ngeun típ **tip (gratuity)**
เงินปลีก ngeun blèek **change (coins)**
เงินมัดจำ ngeun mát jam **deposit**
เงินสด ngeun sòt **cash**

จ

จดหมาย jòt-măi **letter • mail**
จมูก jà-mòok **nose**
จอง jorng **book (make a booking)**
จาน jahn **dish**
จิตรกรรม jìt-drà-gam **painting (the art)**

ใจกลางเมือง jai glahng meu·ang **city centre**

ช

ชนบท chon·ná·bot **countryside**
ช่อง ขายตั๋ว chôrng kăi đŏo·a **ticket office**
ชั้นธุรกิจ chán tú·rá·gìt **business class**
ชั่วโมง chôo·a mohng **hour**
ช้า cháh **late**
ชายแดน chai daan **border**
ชายหาด chai hàht **beach**
ชื่อ chêu **name**
เช็ค chék **cheque • check**
เช็คเดินทาง chék deun tahng **travellers cheque**
เช็คอิน chék in **check-in (desk)**
เช่า chôw **hire • rent**

ซ

ซ่อม sôrm **repair**
ซัก sák **wash (clothes)**
ซื้อของ séu kŏrng **shop**
ซูเปอร์มาร์เก็ต soo·ɓeu·mah·gèt **supermarket**

ด

ดนตรี don·đree **music**
ดนตรีร็อก don·đree rórk **rock (music)**
ด่วน dòo·an **urgent**
ด้วยกัน đôo·ay gan **together**
ดื่ม dèum **drink**
ดื่มน้ำผึ้งพระจันทร์ dèum nám pêung prá jan **honeymoon**
เด็ก dèk **child**
เด็กชาย dèk chai **boy**
เด็กๆ dèk dèk **children**
เดิน deun **walk**
เดินทางธุรกิจ deun tahng tú·rá·gìt **business trip**
เดี๋ยวนี้ dĕe·o née **now**
เดือน deu·an **month**

ต

ตลาด đà·làht **market**
ตลาดน้ำ đà·làht nám **floating market**
ตอนเช้า đorn chów **morning**
ตอนบ่าย đorn bài **afternoon**
ตั๋ว đŏo·a **ticket**
ต่างชาติ đàhng châht **foreign**
ตารางเวลา đah·rahng wair·lah **time-table**
ตำรวจ đam·ròo·at **police**
ตู้เซฟ đôo sép **safe**
ตู้โทรศัพท์ đôo toh·rá·sàp **phone box**
ตู้นอน đôo norn **sleeping car**
ตู้ฝากกระเป๋า đôo fàhk grà·ɓŏw **luggage lockers**
ตู้รับประทานอาหาร đôo ráp ɓrà·tahn ah·hăhn **dining car**
ตู้เอทีเอ็ม đôo air tee em **automated teller machine (ATM)**
เตี้ย đêe·a **short (height)**
เตียง đee·ang **bed**
เตียงคู่ đee·ang kôo **double bed**

ถ

ถ่านไฟฉาย tàhn fai chăi **battery (flashlight)**
ถึง tĕung **to**
ถุง tŭng **bag**
ถุงนอน tŭng norn **sleeping bag**
ถุงยางอนามัย tŭng yahng à·nah·mai **condom**
แถม tăam **complementary (free)**

ท

ทองคำ torng kam **gold**
ทะเบียนรถ tá·bee·an rót **car registration**
ทะเล tá·lair **sea**
ทะเลสาบ tá·lair sàhp **lake**
ทั้งสอง táng sŏrng **both**
ทั้งหมด táng mòt **all**
ทันสมัย tan sà·măi **modern**

85

ทัวร์ too·a **tour • guided tour**

ทาง tahng **path**

ทางด่วน tahng dòo·an **motorway (tollway)**

ทางตรง tahng drong **direct**

ทางหลวง tahng lŏo·ang **highway**

ทาน tahn **eat (polite)**

ทารก tah-rók **baby**

ทำไม tam mai **why**

ทำสะอาด tam sà-àht **clean**

ทำให้ถูกต้อง tam hâi tòok dông **validate**

ทำอาหาร tam ah-hăhn **cook**

ทิวทัศน์ tew tát **view**

ทิศตะวันตก tít đà-wan đòk **west**

ทิศใต้ tít đâi **south**

ทิศเหนือ tít nĕu·a **north**

ที่ têe **at**

ที่ขายขนมปัง têe kăi kà-nŏm bang **bakery**

ที่เขี่ยบุหรี่ têe kèe·a bù·rèe **ashtray**

ที่จอดรถแท็กซี่ têe jòrt rót táak-sêe **taxi stand**

ที่แจ้งของหาย têe jâang kŏrng hăi **lost property office**

ที่ซักผ้า têe sák pâh **laundry (place)**

ที่ทำการไปรษณีย์ têe tam gahn brai-sà-nee **post office**

ที่นั่ง têe nâng **seat (place)**

ที่นี่ têe née **here**

ที่พัก têe pák **accommodation**

ที่รับกระเป๋า têe ráp grà-bŏw **baggage claim**

ที่แล้ว tee láa·ou **last (previous)**

ที่หลัง tee lăng **later**

ที่ไหน têe năi **where**

เที่ยงคืน têe·ang keun **midnight**

เที่ยงวัน têe·ang wan **midday**

เที่ยวกลางคืน têe·o glahng keun **night out**

เที่ยวเดียว têe·o dee·o **one-way (ticket)**

เที่ยวบิน têe·o bin **flight (aeroplane)**

เที่ยวพักผ่อน têe·o pák pòrn **vacation**

โทร toh **telephone**

โทรศัพท์ toh-rá-sàp **telephone**

โทรศัพท์มือถือ toh-rá-sàp meu tĕu **mobile phone**

ธ

ธนาคาร tá-nah-kahn **bank**

ธุรกิจ tú-rá-gìt **business**

น

น้องชาย nórng chai **brother (younger)**

นักศึกษา nák sèuk-săh **student**

น้ำ nám **water**

นางพยาบาล nahng pá-yah-bahn **nurse (female)**

นามสกุล nahm sà-kun **family name • surname**

นาฬิกา nah-lí-gah **watch**

นาฬิกาปลุก nah-lí-gah blùk **alarm clock**

น้ำนม nám nom **milk**

น้ำมัน nám man **oil**

น้ำมันเครื่อง nám man krêu·ang **oil (motor)**

น้ำมันเบนซิน nám-man ben-sin **gas (petrol)**

บ

บน bon **on**

บริษัท bor-rí-sàt **company**

บริษัทท่องเที่ยว bor-rí-sàt tôrng têe·o **travel agency**

บัญชี ban-chee **account**

บัญชีธนาคาร ban-chee tá-nah-kahn **bank account**

บัตรขึ้นเครื่องบิน bàt kêun krêu·ang bin **boarding pass**

บัตรเครดิต bàt crair-dìt **credit card**

บัตรโทรศัพท์ bàt toh-rá-sàp **phone card**

บันได ban-dai **stairway**

บ้านพัก bâhn pák **boarding house**

บ้านเยาวชน bâhn yow-wá-chon **youth hostel**

บิลล์ bin **bill/check (restaurant etc)**

บุรุษพยาบาล bù-rùt pá-yah-bahn **nurse (male)**

บุหรี่ bù·rèe **cigarette**

เบนซิน ben-sin **petrol**

บรก brèk **brakes**
เบียร์ bee·a **beer**
บ่ง bàang **share (with)**
โบสถ์ bòht **church**
ใบกรรมสิทธิ์รถยนต์ bai gam-má-sìt rót yon **car owner's title**
ใบขับขี่ bai kàp kèe **drivers licence**
ใบสั่งยา bai sàng yah **prescription**
ใบเสร็จ bai sèt **receipt**

ป

ประตู bràa-doo **gate (airport, etc)**
ปรับอากาศ bràp ah-gàht **air-conditioned**
ปราสาท bràh-sàht **castle**
ปลอกหมอน blòrk mŏrn **pillowcase**
ป่วย bòo-ay **sick • ill**
ปอนด์ born **pound (money, weight)**
ปัญญาอ่อน ban-yah òrn **idiot**
ปั๊มน้ำมัน bám nám-man **petrol station**
ป้ายรถเมล์ bâi rót mair **bus stop**
ปิกนิก bìk-ník **picnic**
ปิดแล้ว bìt láa-ou **closed**
ปี bee **year**
เป้ bâir **backpack**
เปลี่ยนแปลง blèe-an blaang **change (general)**
แปรง braang **brush**
แปรงสีฟัน braang sěe fan **toothbrush**
ไป bai **go**
ไปกลับ bai glàp **return (ticket)**
ไปข้างนอก bai kâhng nôrk **go out**
ไปซื้อของ bai séu kŏrng **go shopping**
ไปรษณีย์ brai-sà-nee **mail (postal system)**
ไปรษณีย์ทางธรรมดา brai-sà-nee tahng tam-má-dah **surface mail**
ไปรษณียบัตร brai-sà-nee-yá-bàt **postcard**

ผ

ผม pŏm **hair**
ผลไม้ pŏn-lá-mái **fruit**
ผัก pàk **vegetable**

ผ้าเช็ดตัว pâh chét đoo·a **towel**
ผ้าเช็ดปาก pâh chét bàhk **napkin**
ผ้าซัก pâh sák **laundry (clothes)**
ผ้าปูที่นอน pâh boo têe norn **bed linen**
ผ้าลินิน pâh lí-nin **linen (material)**
ผ้าห่ม pâh hòm **blanket**
ผ้าไหม pâh măi **silk**
ผ้าอ้อม pâh ôrm **diaper/nappy**
ผิวเกรียมแดด pěw gree-am dàat **sunburn**
ผู้จัดการ pôo jàt gahn **manager**
ผู้ชาย pôo chai **man**
ผู้โดยสาร pôo doy sǎhn **passenger**
ผู้หญิง pôo yĭng **woman**
เผ็ด pèt **hot (spicy)**
แผนที่ pǎan têe **map**
แผ่นพับโฆษณา pàan páp koh-sà-nah **brochure**

ฝ

ฝน fŏn **rain**
ฝักบัว fàk boo·a **shower**

พ

พจนานุกรม pót-jà-nah-nú-grom **dictionary**
พิกัดน้ำหนักกระเป๋า pí-gàt nám nàk grà-bŏw **baggage allowance**
พิพิธภัณฑ์ pi-pít-tá-pan **museum**
พี่ชาย pêe chai **brother (older)**
เพื่อน pêu·an **friend**

ฟ

ฟรี free **free (gratis)**
ฟิล์ม fim **film (for camera)**
ฟิล์มสไลด์ fim sà-lái **slide (film)**
แฟนผู้ชาย faan pôo chai **boyfriend**
แฟนสาว faan sŏw **girlfriend**
แฟลช flâat **flash (camera)**
ไฟ fai **light (electric)**
ไฟฉาย fai chǎi **torch (flashlight)**
ไฟแช็ก fai cháak **cigarette lighter**

87

ก

ภาพเขียน pâhp kĕe-an **painting (a work)**

ภาษีสนามบิน pah-sĕe sà-nǎhm bin **airport tax**

ภูเขา poo kŏw **mountain**

ม

มีดพับ mêet páp **penknife**

มื้ออาหาร méu ah-hǎhn **meal**

เมา mow **drunk**

เมาคลื่น mow klêun **travel sickness (boat)**

เมาเครื่อง mow krêu·ang **travel sickness (air)**

เมีย mee·a **wife**

เมือง meu·ang **city**

เมื่อไร mêu·a rai **when**

เมื่อวาน mêu·a wahn **yesterday**

เมื่อวานซืน mêu·a wahn seun **day before yesterday**

โมเด็ม moh-dem **modem**

ไม่มี mâi mee **without**

ไม่มีห้องว่าง mâi mee hôrng wâhng **no vacancy**

ไม่สูบบุหรี่ mâi sòop bù-rèe **non-smoking**

ย

ยกทรง yók song **bra**

ยกเลิก yók lêuk **cancel**

ยา yah **medicine (medication)**

ยืนยัน yeun yan **confirm (a booking)**

ยุ่ง yûng **busy**

เย็น yen **cool • cold**

ร

รถเข็น rót kĕn **wheelchair**

รถเข็นเด็ก rót kĕn dèk **stroller**

รถจักรยาน rót jàk-gà-yahn **bicycle**

รถบัส rót bàt **bus (intercity)**

รถมอเตอร์ไซค์ rót mor-đeu-sai **motorcycle**

รถเมล์ rót mair **bus (city)**

รถยนต์ rót yon **car**

ร่วมกันใช้ rôo·am gan chái **share (a dorm etc)**

รหัสไปรษณีย์ rá-hàt brai-sà-nee **post code**

รองเท้า rorng tów **shoe**

ร้อน rórn **hot**

รับประทาน ráp brà-tahn **eat (very formal)**

ราคา rah-kah **price**

ราคาส่วนลด rah-kah sòo·an lót **discount**

ร้าน ráhn **shop**

ร้านกาแฟ ráhn gah-faa **cafe**

ร้านขายของชำ ráhn kǎi kǒrng cham **convenience store**

ร้านขายเนื้อ ráhn kǎi néu·a **butcher's shop**

ร้านขายหนังสือพิมพ์ ráhn kǎi nǎng-sĕu pim **newsagency**

ร้านขายอุปกรณ์เขียน ráhn kǎi ùp-bà-gorn kĕe·an **stationer's (shop)**

ร้านดนตรี ráhn don-đree **music shop**

ร้านเสริมสวย ráhn sĕum sŏo·ay **beauty salon**

ร้านอินเตอร์เนต ráhn in-đeu-nét **Internet cafe**

รายการเดินทาง rai gahn deun tahng **itinerary**

รายวัน rai wan **daily**

รูปหล่อ rôop lòr **handsome**

เรือ reu·a **boat**

เรือข้ามฟาก reu·a kâhm fâhk **ferry**

โรงซักรีด rohng sák rêet **launderette**

โรงพยาบาล rohng pá-yaa-bahn **hospital**

โรงแรม rohng raam **hotel**

ล

ละคร lá-korn **play (theatre)**

ล้าง láhng **wash (something)**

ล่าม lâhm **interpreter**

ฟ์ líp **lift (elevator)**
กชาย lôok chai **son**
กสาว lôok sŏw **daughter**
ก lék **small**
าว le·ou **bad**
ัตถุโบราณ wát·tù boh·rahn **antique**
น wan **day**
ันเกิด wan gèut **birthday**
ันที่ wan têe **date (day)**
ันที่เกิด wan têe gèut **date of birth**
ันนี้ wan née **today**
ันมะรืน wan má·reun **day after
tomorrow**
่าง wâhng **free (available) • vacant**
่ายน้ำ wâi nám **swim**
เวลาเปิด wair·lah bèut **opening hours**
แว่นตา wâan dah **glasses (spectacles)**

ค

ศุลกากร sŭn·lá·gah·gorn **customs**

ส

สกปรก sòk·gà·bròk **dirty**
สถานีขนส่ง sà·tăh·nee kŏn sòng **bus
station**
สถานีตำรวจ sà·tăh·nee đam·ròo·at
police station
สถานีรถไฟ sà·tăh·nee rót fai **train
station**
สถานีรถไฟฟ้า sà·tăh·nee rót fai fáh
metro station
สนามบิน sà·năhm bin **airport**
สบาย sà·bai **comfortable**
สมุดโทรศัพท์ sà·mùt toh·rá·sàp **phone
book**
สรรพสินค้า sàp·pá·sĭn·káh **department store**
สรรพสินค้า sàp·pá·sĭn·káh **shopping
centre**
สระว่ายน้ำ sà wâi nám **swimming pool**
สวน sŏo·an **garden**
สวย sŏo·ay **beautiful**
สองเตียง sŏrng đee·ang **twin beds**

สะอาด sà·àht **clean**
สำนักงานท่องเที่ยว săm·nák ngahn tôrng
têe·o **tourist office**
สีขาว sĕe kŏw **white**
สีเขียว sĕe kĕe·o **green**
สีชมพู sĕe chom·poo **pink**
สีดำ sĕe dam **black**
สีแดง sĕe daang **red**
สีน้ำเงิน sĕe nám ngeun **blue (dark)**
สีน้ำตาล sĕe nám dahn **brown**
สีฟ้า sĕe fáh **blue (light)**
สีส้ม sĕe sôm **orange (colour)**
สีเหลือง sĕe lĕu·ang **yellow**
สุข sùk **happy**
สุขภาพ sù·kà·pâhp **health**
สุขาสาธารณะ sù·kăh săh·tah·rá·ná
public toilet
เสีย sĕe·a **out of order**
เสื้อกันหนาว sêu·a gan nŏw **jacket**
เสื้อคลุม sêu·a klum **coat**
เสื้อเชิ้ต sêu·a chéut **shirt**
เสื้อถัก sêu·a tàk **jumper • sweater**
เสื้อผ้า sêu·a pâh **clothing**
แสตมป์ sà·đaam **stamp**
โสด sòht **single (person)**
ใส่กุญแจแล้ว sài gun·jaa láa·ou **locked**

ห

หนัก nàk **heavy**
หนัง năng **leather**
หนังสือ năng·sĕu **book**
หนังสือเดินทาง năng·sĕu deun tahng
passport
หนังสือพิมพ์ năng·sĕu pim **newspaper**
หน้า nâh **next (month)**
หน้า nâh **season**
หน้าต่าง nâh đàhng **window**
หน้าใบไม้ผลิ nâh bai mái pli **spring
(season)**
หน้าร้อน nâh rórn **summer**
หนาว nŏw **cold (sensation)**
หน้าหนาว nâh nŏw **winter**
หมอ mŏr **doctor**
หมอน mŏrn **pillow**
หมา măh **dog**

89

หมายเลขหนังสือเดินทาง mǎi lêk nǎng-sěu deun tahng **passport number**

หมายเลขห้อง mǎi lêk hôrng **room number**

หลัง lǎng **back (body)**

ห้อง hôrng **room**

ห้องเก็บเสื้อ hôrng gèp sêu·a **cloakroom**

ห้องคู่ hôrng kôo **double room**

ห้องเดี่ยว hôrng dèe·o **single room**

ห้องพักรอ hôrng pák ror **waiting room**

ห้องพักสำหรับคนเดินทางผ่าน hôrng pák sǎm-ràp kon deun tahng pàhn **transit lounge**

ห้องรับฝากกระเป๋า hôrng ráp fàhk grá-ĕow **left luggage (office)**

ห้องว่าง hôrng wâhng **vacancy**

ห้องแสดงภาพ hôrng sà-daang pâhp **art gallery**

หักแล้ว hàk láa·ou **broken**

หัตถกรรม hàt-tà-gam **crafts**

หาย hǎi **lost**

หิวน้ำ hěw nám **thirsty (to be)**

เหรียญ rěe·an **coins**

เหล้า lôw **alcohol**

เหล้าไวน์ lôw wai **wine**

แห้ง hâang **dry**

ใหญ่ yài **big**

ใหญ่กว่า yài gwàh **bigger**

ใหม่ mài **new**

อ

อย่างช้า yàhng cháh **slowly**

อร่อย à-ròy **tasty**

ออกเดินทาง òrk deun tahng **depart (leave)**

อ่างน้ำ àhng nám **bath**

อาทิตย์ ah-tít **week**

อาหารกลางวัน ah-hǎhn glahng wan **lunch**

อาหารมื้อเย็น ah-hǎhn méu yen **dinner**

อาหารว่าง ah-hǎhn wâhng **snack**

อินเตอร์เนต in-deu-nét **Internet**

อุณหภูมิ un-hà-poom **temperature (weather)**

อุ่น ùn **warm**

อุบัติเหตุ ù-bàt-dì-hèt **accident**

ไอ ai **cough**

Acknowledgments
Associate Product Director Angela Tinson
Product Editor Sandie Kestell
Language Writers Bruce Evans, Joe Cummings
Cover Designer Campbell McKenzie
Cover Researcher Gwen Cotter

Thanks
Kate Chapman, Gwen Cotter, James Hardy, Indra Kilfoyle,
Saralinda Turner, Juan Winata

Published by Lonely Planet Global Ltd
CRN 554153

2nd Edition – April 2024
Text © Lonely Planet 2024
Cover Image Damnoen Saduak Floating Market, Ratchaburi;
Visual Storyteller/Shutterstock ©

Printed in China 10 9 8 7 6 5 4 3 2 1

Contact lonelyplanet.com/contact

Although the authors and Lonely Planet try to make the information
as accurate as possible, we accept no responsibility for any loss, injury
or inconvenience sustained by anyone using this book.

Paper in this book is certified against the Forest Stewardship Council™
standards. FSC™ promotes environmentally responsible, socially
beneficial and economically viable management of the world's forests.

Index